WOMEN on
BOARD

"Today, more and more corporate boards are recognizing that gender diversity is a business imperative and a critical element in sustaining successful enterprises. Increasing the number of women in leadership positions has to be a priority, not only because it is the right thing to do, but also because it is essential to building a high performance organization. We have the highest female representation on KPMG's U.S. board in our history, and we know it makes us a stronger organization. Diversity in senior leadership is important in achieving the inclusive culture we strive for at KPMG."

> – **John Veihmeyer,** Global Chairman of KPMG and Chairman and CEO of KPMG in the U.S.

"Women's presence in the boardroom in now mandatory for every top-tier global company. This new book not only lays out the case, it provides a roadmap for high-performing women leaders to join high-performing boards. It is a must-read for every sitting board director, man or woman, and for everyone who aspires to a corporate board seat."

> – **Sandi Peterson,** Group Worldwide Chairman of Johnson & Johnson and a director of Dun & Bradstreet

"There are a lot of "how to" books on how to secure a board seat. Nancy and Susan's book cuts through the clutter and provides a thoughtful and detailed primer to create a personal board career road map for success. I encourage anyone thinking about joining a board to carefully study these pages, earmark them and refer to the action tables and anecdotes for inspiration and useful information. This is a practical and helpful book."

> – **Maryellen Gleason,** former President and Executive Director of Milwaukee Symphony Orchestra and a director of WPO/YPO Wisconsin

"This book has it all- insider secrets from top Female Board Directors plus key findings from well-respected research sources from around the world delivered in a digestible entertaining format. As co-founder of WomenCorporateDirectors (WCD), Susan Stautberg shares her unique access to world business leaders and a truly global perspective on best practices for board diversity. Together with Nancy Calderon, a global lead partner at KPMG, one of the largest professional services companies in the world, *Women on Board* provides the most comprehensive resource on why board diversity is more than a moral imperative, it's a business imperative!"

> – **Cynthia Cleveland,** a director of CPP (The Myers Briggs Company), an advisory board member of Indiana University, a trustee of the Center for Economic Development and the Chair of the Women's YPO network

"Women aspiring to board positions – and all who are champions of change for greater gender equity on boards – will want to study this book, which provides important insights, and specific tactical advice. Marsh & McLennan Companies is proud to support WomanCorporateDirectors as it champions women directors and best practices in board governance around the world."

> – **Nicole Gardner,** VP, Chief Diversity and Inclusion Officer of Marsh & McLennan Companies

"Ten years ago when I joined my first corporate board, most CEOs still scratched their heads, shrugged their shoulders, and gave up on identifying women directors—there simply were not enough "sitting women CEOs" to go around. Much has changed in the past decade as increased competitive pressure for talent has pushed board search committees to think more broadly about the vast pool of female leaders with the requisite talent, smarts, creativity, and vision so needed in the 21st century global boardroom. WCD has played a significant role in changing the boardroom mix; it serves as a vital network for those of us already at the table, as an educator of prospective women directors, and as a leading advocate of best practices in corporate governance. Women on Board is a valuable resource for current officers, sitting directors and those who aspire to serve."

> – **Connie K. Duckworth,** Founder and CEO of ARZU, Inc., retired Partner and Managing Director of Goldman Sachs, and a corporate director

"At Spencer Stuart we believe board composition is at the heart of board effectiveness and are committed to helping develop and identify a qualified, diverse slate of candidates. We share Women Corporate Directors' goal of building the female executive pipeline by identifying seasoned and first time qualified women directors and supporting their preparation for director service."

> – Julie Daum, North American Board Services Practice Leader and a director of Spencer Stuart, and a director of Seacoast Banking Corporation

"To think of WCD as another women's organization is to ignore its repercussions. WCD has been a game changer in places like Saudi Arabia and other Gulf States as well as Asia and Latin America. WCD is empowering women by giving them a much needed strong and confident voice. In fact, women who have been culturally marginalized now have a platform that will inevitably lead to changes in public policy."

> – Marsha "Marty" Evans, Rear Admiral, U.S. Navy (Ret.), Director of Weight Watchers International, Inc., and, The North Highland Company and co-chair of the WCD North Florida and South Georgia Chapter

"When you look around and see a whole range of women from around the world who have come together unapologetically about the real need to have greater inclusion of women in corporate boardrooms—the spirit of collaboration that this group brings—it is just so overwhelmingly supportive."

> – Dr. Helene Gayle, MD, MPH, President and CEO CARE USA, Director of The Coca Cola Company and The Colgate Palmolive Company

"I am overwhelmed with the positive response I received from the stellar group of women—who have even greater stories to tell."

> – Fatin Bundagji, President of the TLC Management & Development Consultancy and director of the Jeddah Chamber of Commerce and Industry

"In Brazil, WCD's main accomplishments include: raising the awareness in the women business community about the lack of women on board roles; preparing women to be qualified to sit on these boards, not only through formal education—such as studying governance and capital market matters—but also through informal networking; and encouraging companies and top decision makers towards diversity and the benefits of having women on boards."

> – **Ana Paula Chagas,** Managing Partner of 2GET Executive Search, President of the Senior Advisory Board of the Nature Conservancy in Brazil, and co-chair of WCD Sao Paulo Chapter

"One of the joys of expanding WCD's mandate internationally is bringing together the significant and growing class of women business leaders and entrepreneurs. "I am Nigerian and I am proud!" was a leitmotiv of the week's activities—a four day long dazzling display of seminars, teach ins, and social events, all hosted by women who were eager for the international recognition of a chapter. The Middle East and Africa are regions where WCD chapters can make a historic contribution to the rising prominence of female business leaders. The international recognition and thought leadership which WCD brings to their work is truly appreciated for what it can do to help them realize their own trail blazing goals."

> – **Frances Cook,** former Ambassador to Oman and to the Republic of Cameroon, a former director at Arlington Associates Limited, and former chair of Lonrho PLV and the Ballard Group

"The WCD Italy Chapter has gathered the most influential and capable women in the country. Currently, its members represent more than 28 percent of overall market cap of the Italian stock exchange. This is an even more significant result considering that there are still listed companies with no women on board, which make up over 25 percent of market cap."

> — **Marina Brogi,** Deputy Dean Faculty of Economics Sapienza Università di Roma, director of Salini-Impregilo and Ubi Banca, co-chair of WCD Milan Chapter and advisory board member of WCD

"You are doing a great job at helping women and I'm sure this is helpful not only for corporations but society."

> — **Maurice Levy,** Chairman and CEO, Publicis Groupe

"The more I leaned into the championing of equal opportunity, I also found that it was in the self interest of organizations to search out and advance capable women, as those organizations seemed to prosper and perform at a higher level when they fully leveraged the diversity of their resource base."

> — **Doug Conant,** Chairman of Avon Products, founder and CEO of ConantLeadership, chairman of Kellogg Executive Leadership Institute of Northwestern University and former president and CEO of Campbell Soup Company

"This is truly a group of people that is generating impact on people around them and on the world."

> — **Sophia Wang,** Vice President of Marketing & Special Initiative of Genpact Asia

"There's no question that one of the greatest forces of the 21st century will be women's economic empowerment around the world. As more women start their own businesses, participate on corporate boards, and lead companies, governments and civil society organizations, we will not only create a more just world, but a healthier, safer, and more sustainable world as well. The Coca Cola Company benefits enormously from the leadership of our four women board members. WomenCorporateDirectors is an important catalyst in this movement, and one we're proud to support through the active engagement of two of our senior women leaders at Coca Cola—Ceree Eberly, our Chief People Officer, and Beatriz Perez, our Chief Sustainability Officer."

> – **Muhtar Kent,** Chairman and Chief Executive Officer, The Coca Cola Company

"Networking through WomenCorporateDirectors does actually make a difference. The increasing number of women in the boardrooms of the world's companies is an unstoppable and important global movement. It makes economic sense."

> – **Jane Diplock** Director of Singapore Exchange Limited, International Integrated Reporting Council Board, and Australian Financial Services Group Pty Limited

"You can count on Nancy Calderon and Susan Stautberg's Women On Board for the most insightful thinking and set of recommendations on transforming corporate boardrooms. They tell it straight about what's needed to get to the higher ground of great leadership and great corporate governance for the era ahead."

> – **James Kristie,** Editor and Associate Publisher, *Directors & Boards*

"Susan realizes that corporate board diversity is more than an ideal, and that one passionate person could gather an army to change how corporations perceive leadership and the role of women. She sees diversity as a business imperative. Susan is an extraordinary leader and champions tough issues, with courage and humor. She is not only a globally recognized leader in corporate governance and diversity on boards, but she has changed the tone of our civil discourse. She has helped to change the composition of boards so that more diverse voices are making a difference around the table, in the world and for the world."

– **Henrietta Fore,** Chairman and CEO of Holsman International, co-chair of the Asia Society, director of Exxon Mobil Corporation, Aspen Institute, General Mills, Theravance Biopharma, Inc., Seaward International Company, Committee for Economic Development, and Stockton Products, and advisory board member and global co-chair of WCD

"Corporations with women directors on their boards perform better than those with all-male boards, according to the Credit Suisse six-year research study (2012). Susan Stautberg single-handedly fueled momentum years before when she launched WomenCorporateDirectors around her dining room table in 2001. Gender diversity on boards has now become a national imperative among shareholders, institutional investors, and public opinion. Thanks to Susan's bold leadership—WCD has expanded globally to engage women directors and male CEOs. This action-packed book is a testament to what can and will be done by enlightened corporations from here forward, and shows women how to forge their careers toward the ultimate goal."

– **Betsy Berkhemer-Credaire,** President and co-founder of Berkhemer Clayton Retained Executive Search, author of The Board Game—How Smart Women Become Corporate Directors and co-chair of WCD Los Angeles Chapter

"Susan's leadership has built WCD into a global educational community of trust and knowledge. Her achievements and refusal to settle for once "traditional" roles will change the lives of leaders for generations to come, and we will be a better and stronger country as a result...Susan is passionately dedicated to the advancement of women and to diversity. We all benefit when those who lead us also reflect us in terms of gender, color, nationality and more. The young gain role models, students have mentors, customers feel understood and we are all better for being part of a multi-colored tapestry. It is especially important that young women have strong entrepreneurial role models and mentors. Susan saw this need years ago, but unlike so many others, she acted."

— **Maggie Wilderotter,** Chairman and CEO of Frontier Communications Corporation and director of Xerox Corporation and Procter & Gamble

"As Marriott International celebrates the 15th anniversary of our Women's Leadership Initiative, we are proud partners with WomenCorporateDirectors and Susan Stautberg.

Companies flourish when women have opportunities and professional development to fill leadership positions, including those in the C-Suite and Board Room. That's where WCD and Susan Stautberg are playing an invaluable role as they give women the tools to thrive and lead."

— **Kathleen Matthews,** Executive Vice President Global Communications and Public Affairs of Marriott International

WOMEN on BOARD

insider secrets

to getting on a board and succeeding as a director

By Nancy Calderon
Susan Stautberg

Books may be purchased in quantity and/or special sales by contacting:
WomenCorporateDirectors
P.O. Box 7487
West Palm Beach, FL 33405
Email: womenonboard@womencorporatedirectors.com
Web Address: http://www.womencorporatedirectors.com/?page=_WomenOnBoard

Cover Design: Alternatives NYC
Interior Design: Lentini Design & Marketing, Inc.
Indexer: Denise Carlson
Publishing House: Quotation Media

First Printing, 2014
ISBN 978-0-692-26294-8
Printed in the United States of America

Dedication

"Do not go where the path may lead, go instead where there is no path and leave a trail."

– Ralph Waldo Emerson

This book is dedicated to the women around the world who create new paths while sponsoring and mentoring others to create more champions of change; as well as to our families who have given us the support to be path finders.

To Phil Calderon, Lindsey Calderon, Ted Stautberg, Edward Stautberg, Alison Stautberg and our personal boards of directors:

For everything that comes next
For believing in us
For your willingness to laugh and love
For sharing victories and defeats
For your endless support
For giving deeper meaning to family
For providing new horizons
For choosing the higher road
For knowing every path has puddles
For being my foundation
For your unfailing support

It's your turn, it's our time.

Global companies (and just about every company is global nowadays) compete with everyone, everywhere, for everything. To do that, they need the best talent. Legendary investor Warren Buffett has said that one reason for his success is that he was competing with only half the population. Put another way, keeping women out of the game creates an uneven playing field.

At the same time, we live in an age when education, empathy, and social sensitivity are increasingly important. Women — with their adaptability, people skills, intelligence, and long-term focus — are shaping the modern world. If genius is recognizing the obvious before anyone else, stupidity is the failure to do anything about the obvious. So, we decided to write this book to give women the information and encouragement they need to set their sights on a seat at the directors' table.

Certainly, women can bring to a board the same qualifications as men should to a board: honesty and integrity, a deeply-felt commitment to good work, intellectual curiosity, and an ability to "think big" about strategy, markets (both global and local), and emerging opportunities. They also bring competitive skills and experience, not just in finance but also in other business areas and in leadership itself.

But we like to think that women also bring something particular to a board, some quality of character and behavior that comes from their unique paths to professional success — paths that often differ from those of their male peers.

A new paradigm is emerging as boards begin to reflect more accurately on the diversity in society at large, in universities, and in corporations large and small. The traditional board of 12 like minded men with similar backgrounds and experiences who all think the same way is feeling out-of-date and out-of-touch. The right diversity in the boardroom connects a company with new customers and shareholders.

To write this book, we asked both men and women executives and board directors, each of them a champion of change, to contribute their insights and anecdotes. Their perspectives are enriching, enlightening, and entertaining. Let's keep the conversation going: we welcome your questions, comments, and success stories.

Nancy Calderon
Global Lead Partner, KPMG LLP
Director, KPMG's Global Delivery Center, India

Susan Stautberg
Founder and President, PartnerCom Corporation
CEO and Co-chair of WomenCorporateDirectors
Co-founder of OnBoard Bootcamp

About this book

In this book, you'll find "need to know" observations that are useful for any woman with board ambitions. Each is a stand-alone thought, so you can read the book from cover to cover or jump around as your interest and curiosity dictate. In writing the book, we drew on content from the following sources:

The personal ideas, anecdotes, and provocative opinions of members of WomenCorporateDirectors (WCD), the only global membership organization and community of women on corporate boards, as well as those of some male CEOs known as champions of change. While WCD is headquartered in the United States, most of its chapters are in other countries and on other continents. This global reach affirms our belief that no one governance model fits all organizations: we all need to listen to and learn from others.

With more than 3,500 members who serve on more than 6,500 boards in 66 chapters around the world, WCD provides members a unique opportunity for networking, making new friends, and learning from the intellectual capital of accomplished women serving on global boards. WCD challenges every business leader to bring more women onto corporate boards and to build diverse boards that are multi-gender, multi-skilled, multi-national, multi-ethnic, and multi-generational.

Data and analysis from the research of WCD and Heidrick & Struggles, including the *2012 Board of Directors Survey*, conducted by Boris Groysberg, PhD, the Richard

P. Chapman Professor of Business Administration at the Harvard Business School, and Deborah Bell, organizational behavior expert and researcher, and the WCD and Heidrick & Struggles *2013 Board of Directors Survey: The State of Leadership Succession Planning Today.* In our annual survey, we ask male and female directors qualitative and quantitative questions about trends, attitudes, and progress (or the lack thereof) relative to the role of women in corporate governance.

The extensive experience of KPMG, one of the largest professional services companies in the world with 155,000 professionals in 155 countries, Spencer Stuart, one of the world's leading executive search consulting firms, and Pearl Meyer & Partners, a leading executive compensation consulting firm serving top management, boards and compensation committees.

We're strong believers in the value of asking questions. As Andrew Sobel and Jerold Panas write in their terrific book, *Power Questions: Build Relationships, Win New Business, and Influence Others,* "Good questions are often more powerful than answers. Good questions challenge your thinking and reframe and redefine the problem. They throw cold water on our most dearly held assumptions and force us out of our traditional thinking. They motivate us to learn and discover more. They remind us of what is most important in our lives." Throughout this book, we ask and suggest that you ask questions. The only caveat we offer is this: there is never just one right answer.

Acknowledgements

We'd like to thank these members and friends of WomenCorporateDirectors for their generous contributions to this book. Each is a remarkable leader and advocate for women.

Zelma Acosta-Rubio, General Counsel, Board's Secretary and a director of Corporate Affairs/CSR at Banco Interbacional del Perú - Interbank, and a director of La Fiduciaria, Intertítulos, Churromania, ProMujer Perú and Vida Perú

Cathy Allen, Chairman and CEO of The Santa Fe Group, a director of El Paso Electric Company and Synovus, an advisory board member of WCD, appointed by President Obama to the Valles Caldera Trust Board and co-chair of WCD Greater New Mexico Chapter

Yolanda Auza, an entrepreneur of Librerias Wilborada 1047, an advisory board member of Engineering School Universidad de los Andes and WCD, and co-chair of WCD Colombia Chapter

Jan Babiak, an independent director of Walgreens, Bank of Montreal and Experian and co-chair of WCD Tennessee Chapter

Sherry Barrat, retired Vice Chairman of Northern Trust Corporation, a director of NextEra Energy, Inc., Prudential Insurance Funds and Arthur J. Gallagher & Co., and an advisory board member of WCD

Melanie Barstad, retired President of Acute Care of Johnson & Johnson and a director of CINTAS and Auburn University Foundation

Deborah Bell, organizational behavior expert and researcher at the Harvard Business School

Betsy Berkhemer-Credaire, President and co-founder of Berkhemer Clayton Retained Executive Search, author of *The Board Game—How Smart Women Become Corporate Directors* and co-chair of WCD Los Angeles Chapter

Anne Berner, CEO of Vallila Interior, a director of Koskisen Oy, Kährs PLC and European Family Businesses in Brussels, co-chair of WCD Family Business Council and co-chair of WCD Finland Chapter

Eleanor Bloxham, CEO of The Value Alliance and Corporate Governance Alliance and co-chair of WCD Columbus Chapter

Marina Brogi, Deputy Dean Faculty of Economics at Sapienza Università di Roma, a director of Salini-Impregilo and Ubi Banca, co-chair of WCD Milan Chapter and an advisory board member of WCD

Martha Finn Brooks, retired President and COO of Novelis, Inc. and a director of Bombardier, Jabil, Inc., and Algeco Scotsman

Fatin Yousef Bundagji, President of the TLC Management & Development Consultancy and a director of the Jeddah Chamber of Commerce and Industry

Phyllis Campbell, Chairman of the Pacific Northwest of JPMorgan, lead director of Alaska Air Group, a director of Nordstrom and Vice Chair of Asia for WCD

Carolyn Chan, an independent consultant and former founding co-chair of the WCD Singapore Chapter

Cynthia Cohen, Founder and President of Strategic Mindshare, a director of Equity One and Steiner Leisure Service, a trustee of the Committee for Economic Development, an advisory board member of AnswerLab, DigiWorksCorp, Sophelle, and WCD and co-chair of WCD New York Chapter

Doug Conant, Chairman of Avon Products, Founder and CEO of ConantLeadership, Chairman of Kellogg Executive Leadership Institute of Northwestern University and former President and CEO of Campbell Soup Company

Frances Cook, former Ambassador to Oman and to the Republic of Cameroon, a former director at Arlington Associates Limited, and former chair of Lonrho PLV and the Ballard Group

Julie Daum, North American Board Services Practice Leader and a director of Spencer Stuart, and a director of Seacoast Banking Corporation

Evelyn Dilsaver, a director of Aeropostale, Tempur Sealy, and Blue Shield of California and an advisory board member of Protiviti

Barbara Duganier, a director of Buckeye Partners, L.P. and a director and National Board Chair of Genesys Works

Ann Dunwoody, retired General in the United States Army and a director of L-3, LMI Logistics Management Institute, Republic Services Group and Council of Trustees Association of United States Army

Elaine J. Eisenman, PhD, Dean and Professor of Management practice of Babson Executive Education and a director of DSW and Harvard Vanguard Medical Associates, co-chair of WCD Boston Chapter and an advisory board member of WCD

Denise Fletcher, a director of Unisys, Inovalon, and Le Groupe Mazars

Henrietta Fore, Chairman and CEO of Holsman International, co-chair of the Asia Society, a director of Exxon Mobil Corporation, Aspen Institute, General Mills, Theravance Biopharma, Inc., Seaward International Company, Committee for Economic Development, and Stockton Products, and an advisory board member and global co-chair of WCD

Alice Gast, a director at Chevron and incoming president of Imperial College in London

Michelle Goldberg, a Partner at Ignition, and a director at Moz, Glympse, Visible Technologies, and UCDS

Sir Gerry Grimstone, Chairman of Standard Life plc and TheCityUK, lead non-executive director of the Ministry of Defence and an independent director of Deloitte LLP

Boris Groysberg, PhD, the Richard P. Chapman Professor of Business Administration at the Harvard Business School

Bonnie Gwin, Vice Chairman and Managing Partner of North America Board of Directors Practice of Heidrick & Struggles and a director of Georgetown University Board of Regents

Kathy Hopinkah Hannan, National Managing Partner of Diversity and Corporate Responsibility for KPMG and chair of KPMG's Diversity Advisory Board, trustee of the Committee for Economic Development, and an advisory board member of Catalyst and Steptoe & Johnson LLP

Darrin Hartzler, Global Manager of Corporate Governance Unit of International Finance Corporation

Chad Holliday, retired Chair and CEO of DuPont, a director of Deere & Co., Royal Dutch Shell, and CH2MHILL and chair of Bank of America

Fatima Al Jaber, a director and the Head of Projects Committee of Al Jaber Group, Chairperson of Al Bashayer Investment Company PJSC, Abu Dhabi Businesswomen's Council and UAE Businesswomen's Council, a director of Abu Dhabi Chamber of Commerce and Industry and Abu Dhabi Council for Economic Development, and chair of the WCD Gulf Cooperation Council Chapter

Shirley Ann Jackson, PhD, President of Rensselaer Polytechnic Institute, and a director of IBM, FedEx, Marathon Oil, Medtronic, and PSEG

Donna James, Managing Director of Lardon & Associates, LLC and director of L Brands, Time Warner Cable, Marathon Petroleum Corporation, and FIS Group

Eileen Kamerick, CFO of Press Ganey Associates, Inc. and a director of Associated Bancorp Westell Technologies, and Legg Mason & Co., LLC

Jill Kanin-Lovers, a director of Heidrick & Struggles, Dot Foods, and Homeownership, and an advisory board member of WCD

James Kristie, Editor and Associate publisher of *Directors & Boards* and an advisory board member of the Center for Corporate Governance of Drexel University

LouAnn Layton, Managing Director of Marsh & McLennan Companies and a director of FIVER

Anne Lim-Obrien, Vice Chairman at Heidrick & Struggles

Wendy Luhabe, Chairman of Women Private Equity Fund and a director of BMW South Africa, International Management Development in Switzerland, and Abraaj Group in Dubai

Namane Magau, Executive Director and owner of B&D Solutions and a director of AON South Africa, Agility Health Care Solutions and Crowie Holdings

Kathy Matsui, Managing Director and Chief Japan Strategist of Goldman Sachs

Pat McKay, a Partner and Managing Director of Templeton & Company LLP, a trustee of Committee for Economic Development, an advisory board member and CFO of WCD and co-chair of WCD South Florida Chapter

Melissa Means, Managing Director at Pearl Meyer & Partners

Denise Morrison, President, CEO and director of Campbell Soup Company, and a director of MetLife, Inc. and Catalyst

Usha Rao-Monari, a director and CEO of Global Water Development Partners, a Blackstone Portfolio Company

Nancy Tuor Moore, retired Group President and director of CH2M HILL, a director of Keller Plc, and on the board of governors of Colorado State University

Carol Nelson, a director of Washington State Department of Revenue and Seattle University

Judi North, a director of Acuity Brands, Community Health Systems, and Lumos Networks, co-chair of WCD Atlanta Chapter and an advisory board member of WCD

Merle Okawara, a former director of Avon Products (Japan), Chairman of JC Comsa Corporation, a director of Parco and co-chair of WCD Japan Chapter

Susan Oliver, Chair of Scale Investors Ltd, and retired Chair of Fusion Retail Brands

Margaret Pederson, President of Amirexx, a director of Viad, Xamax Industries, and TextureMedia, Inc., and an advisory board member of WCD

Sandra Peterson, Group Worldwide Chairman of Johnson & Johnson and a director of Dun & Bradstreet

Liane Pelletier, a director of Expeditors International and Atlantic Tele Network, lead director of Washington Federal, and Chair of Icicle Seafoods

Paul Polman, CEO and executive director of Unilever, Chair of the World Business Council of Sustainable Development, and a director of the UN Global Compact Paul and the Dow Chemical Company

Val Rahmani, a director of Teradici Corporation and Decooda International, Inc.

Nancy Reardon, an independent director of KidsII, co-chair of WCD Philadelphia Chapter and an advisory board member of WCD

Susan Rector, a director of Peoples Bancorp, Inc. and the National Association of Peoples Bank

K. Sue Redman, President of Redman Advisors LLC and Executive Professor of Texas A&M University

Susan Remmer Ryzewic, President, CEO, and a director of EHR Investments, Inc., a director of Endless Pools, Inc., and William Smith Enterprises, Inc. and co-chair of WCD Family Business Council and co-chair of WCD North Florida and South Georgia Chapter

Teresa Ressel, former CEO of UBS Securities and a director of ON Semiconductor Corp

Ellen B. Richstone, a director of eMagin Corporation, Bioamber Inc., Paxeramed Corp, and Pro Teck Valuation Services

Judy B. Rosener, a professor at University of California Irvine's Paul Merage School of Business

Larraine Segil, a director of Frontier Communications, trustee of Committee for Economic Development and Southwestern School of Law, and an advisory board member of UCLA Anderson School of Management and Kandela, Inc.

Clara Shih, CEO and Founder of Hearsay Social and a director of Starbucks Corporation

Stephanie Sonnabend, Co-founder and Chair of 2020 Women on Boards, former CEO and President of Sonesta International Hotels Corporation and a director of Century Bank, Century Bancorp, and Sperry Van Ness

Pernille Spiers-Lopez, former President of IKEA US and a director of Coop, Dk and Meijer, Inc.

Kathryn Swintek, General Partner of Golden Seeds Fund 2 and a director of Turtle & Hughes, Inc., Open Road Integrated Media, Inc., and Mela Sciences, Inc.

Marcy Syms, Partner and President of TPD Group LLC, and a director of Rite Aid

Davia Temin, President and CEO of Temin and Company, Inc., and an advisory board member of WCD

Myla Villanueva, CEO of Novare Technologies, Founder and Managing Director of MDI Group Holdings, and co-chair of WCD Philippines Chapter

Suzy Walton, PhD, Board Deputy Chairman of Manufactures and Commerce (RSA), a director of the Institute of Directors, a director and Chairman of Medical Services Committee, Combat Stress, and member of State Honours Committee

Lulu Wang, a director of MetLife Insurance Company and Asia Society, Overseer of Columbia Business School, an advisory council member of U.S. Trust, and an advisory board member of WCD

Ralph Ward, Publisher of *Boardroom INSIDER*, editor of *The Corporate Board* magazine and author of *Boardroom Q&A*

Edie Weiner, Chairman of Weiner, Edrich, Brown, Inc., and a former corporate director

Maggie Wilderotter, Chairman and CEO of Frontier Communications Corporation, a director of Xerox Corporation and Procter & Gamble, and co-chair of the WCD Global Nominating Commission

Deborah Wince-Smith, President of the Global Federation of Competitiveness Councils, a director of NanoMech, and Vice Chair of Thought Leadership and an advisory board member of WCD

Alison Winter, CEO of Braintree Holdings LLC, Co-founder and an advisory board member of WCD and a director of Nordstrom, Inc. and Blain's Supply

Fritzi Woods, the late, a former director of Jamba Juice and Ignite Restaurants

Kyung Yoon, Founder and CEO of Talent Age Associates, Co-founder and Partner of Executive Board Exchange, a director of MCM Worldwide/Sungjoo Group, and former Chairman and President of Asia America MultiTechnology Association

Please note that each one of these executives has been quoted numerous times throughout the book. For content that is attributed to them, we will include all their affiliations on the first reference. On subsequent references, they will be identified only by name.

We would like to thank Catalina Bustamante, Maggie Hoag, Judy Macdonald and Debbie Milburn for all of their support in helping us to both write and produce this book.

Table of Contents

"The secret of getting ahead is getting started."

– Mark Twain

Like any other endeavor, winning a seat on a corporate board is a journey. And in the words of Lao Tzu, "A journey of a thousand miles begins with a single step." Preparation begins with learning. When it comes to women on boards, what's the status quo? With eyes open, you can anticipate and overcome obstacles in your path. This section shares facts you need to know as you get started.

"I started thinking about board work more than a decade before I joined one. Starting in my late 30s, when I would use search firms to hire talent for my own team, I sought their advice on what I should do to make myself an attractive board candidate when the time was right. I also offered them access to my network anytime they wanted to contact me for ideas for board candidates. As it turns out, one of the search firms I went to for guidance ended up approaching me for ideas on candidates for an opportunity that matched my experience perfectly, and it was around the time I was ready to move to a board portfolio."

Jan Babiak
an independent director of Walgreens,
Bank of Montreal and Experian
and co-chair of WCD Tennessee Chapter

THE STATUS QUO

A CORPORATE DIRECTOR IS, FIRST AND FOREMOST, A LEADER

"Leaders come in many forms, with many styles. There are quiet leaders and leaders one can hear in the next county. Some find strength in eloquence, some in judgment, some in courage."

– John Gardner

What qualities make a board member "good"? With the global economy at a crossroads, it's more important than ever that board directors have the courage to see the world and their corporations realistically, but also with the audacity and skill sets to reimagine and then rebuild both. We need performance, not just promises; action, not just talk.

Like all leaders, board members need integrity, business acumen, curiosity, open-mindedness, a strategic perspective, skills in problem solving and crisis management, and an ability to adapt gracefully. They need to listen well, rising above the noise to interpret dynamic situations, adjusting readily to changing circumstances, and helping their companies stretch to meet the unfamiliar without sacrificing the trust of shareholders, customers, and employees. They also need to be motivators who bring out the best in others, moving people and groups forward purposefully and productively.

That said, we think some important qualities of leadership are found more commonly in women.

Women leaders are expert managers of themselves and their relationships with others. Consequently, they're masters of influence (in a good way). They bestow credit generously, shoulder blame responsibly, and put the group before themselves. Generally speaking, women pay close attention to their environments, often considering leadership a form of service, not an ego trip. Women are more likely than men to be empathic toward and nurturing of others. They're also more likely to create a culture of shared values and solidarity.

"Having emotional intelligence is critical. If a leader is not attuned into other people's needs, he or she cannot be effective. While there's not one type of leadership style that fits every situation, ethics and authenticity are always required," says Kathy Hopinkah Hannan, National Managing Partner of Diversity and Corporate Responsibility for KPMG and chair of KPMG's Diversity Advisory Board, trustee of the Committee for Economic Development, and an advisory board member of Catalyst and Steptoe & Johnson LLP.

"Leadership isn't about running a company; it's about leading people so they can lead *their* people. When a leader influences and inspires, she gets much more done, more quickly. That's why I tell younger women, 'Take time. Start to build relationships. Get to know people *as people.*' Results may be the rite of passage in business, but building relationships gets you the rest of the way."

Denise Morrison | President, CEO and director of Campbell Soup Company, and a director of MetLife, Inc. and Catalyst

BOARD MEMBERS WEAR MANY HATS

"A company's board of directors provides the company with direction and advice. It ensures that the company fulfills its mission statement and, in doing so, frequently sets the company's overall policy objectives ... A well functioning board acts as a top level advisor to the company ... A good board of directors will also let the company know when it is drifting away from its goals and objectives."

— www.wiseGeek.com

While it's hard to keep up with the pace of change today (let alone get ahead of the curve), the price of falling behind just keeps get higher. The stakes — financial, social, environmental, and political — are rising year after year. Of course there's never "one best way" to direct a company's course, but there's always a "better" way.

To do its job — especially in today's complex, global business environment — a board needs people that cover many different kinds of competencies, skills, knowledge, professional experiences, and personal qualities. Some of the newer (and hence less conventional) qualities that might be sought in a director include an understanding of social media and other new technologies, experience in global markets, an appreciation of customer relationship management, and a track record of innovation.

As a group, the board should understand the company's strategies, markets, customers, operations, financial condition, and regulatory environments. As a company changes over time, so should its board's composition. This is one reason why diversity of ethnicity, gender, age, skills sets, and regions of the world is so important today, and why it will be only more important in the future. Simply said, diversity brings new, relevant perspectives to the decision-making process — perspectives that resonate with an increasingly global customer population. Boards should also conduct an annual skill audit to find any gaps in experience and/or diversity that could hinder future success and progress. Planning ahead for board transitions/retirements is just as important as planning ahead for a CEO transition.

In the *Directors & Boards* article, "How to Get on a Board," by Jim Kristie, Editor and Associate publisher of *Directors & Boards* and an advisory board member of the Center for Corporate Governance of Drexel University, Norman Augustine, former chairman and CEO of Lockheed Martin, defines an individual's work when considering board service:

"Why do you want to join a corporate board? If the answer is for self-aggrandizement or prestige, the reputational risks far outweigh any such benefits. Similarly, if it is for financial reward, there are easier, far less risky ways to make money. And if it is because you have a 'cause' to promote, you are not a good board candidate because your role as a director will not be to represent a single interest, but to represent the interests of shareholders as a whole."

Once you join a board, you've made a commitment to take an active role in governing the company. Board directors walk a fine line between actively governing and micro-managing. Essentially, the board provides direction, oversight, and advice. As a board member, you're also responsible for the supervision and evaluation of the CEO. But most importantly, you represent shareholders and work to ensure that the business delivers sustainable, long-term value for them. That's why one of a director's obligations is to ask questions that could shed light on risks and vulnerabilities, as well as opportunities.

In all this work, one thread pulls through: a board must be independent from management.

"Boards are strong, high functioning work groups, whose members trust and challenge one another and engage directly with senior managers on critical issues facing corporations ... What distinguishes exemplary boards is that they are robust, effective, social systems."   Jeffrey A. Sonnenfeld, Associate Dean for Executive Education programs at the Yale School of Management

WE TALK TO A DIVERSITY CHAMPION: DARRIN HARTZLER

Darrin Hartzler serves as Global Manager of the Corporate Governance Unit of International Finance Corporation (IFC), a company committed to ending extreme global poverty by 2030.

In FY13, IFC invested $18.3 billion in 612 projects, of which $6.6 billion went to the poorest countries eligible to borrow from the World Bank's International Development Association. The organization also mobilized an additional $6.5 billion to support the private sector in developing countries. IFC now has a $50 billion portfolio of investment commitments spanning nearly 2,000 companies in 126 countries.

› Why and how is IFC promoting gender diversity on boards around the world?

"Prosperity and diversity go hand-in-hand. By 2015, we expect to fill at least 30 percent of IFC-nominated director positions with women. We'll get there one step at a time.

"For example, in Bosnia/Herzegovina/Serbia, IFC worked with researchers to identify why there are so few women on boards and then used the insights we gained to develop policy recommendations and training programs. In Kosovo, we're working with RTC Consulting, whose CEO is a woman, to implement a three-day program empowering young women to design and implement personal development plans that also address corporate governance improvements in the companies where they work.

"In Jordan, IFC collaborated with the Jordanian Institute of Directors to examine gender diversity in boardrooms among 237 publicly-listed companies and 996 privately-held companies. Our intent was to raise awareness about the ways diversity positively influences an organization's performance. Here, the health industry has the highest female representation on boards with about 11 percent, followed by seven percent in the education sector. In banks' boardrooms, only five percent of directors are women, in insurance companies, only four percent, and financial services sectors, only four percent.

"In Morocco, IFC collaborated with the Ministry for General Affairs, UN Women, the Moroccan Institute of Directors, and the Moroccan Chapter of WomenCorporateDirectors to conduct and disseminate research on the number of women on corporate boards. According to the report, only seven percent of board directors are women, while boards of listed companies fare slightly better at ten percent.

"IFC has hosted workshops in board diversity — in Bangladesh, Yemen, Kosovo, and many other countries —whose purpose includes awareness-raising and capacity-building. These initiatives typically include collaboration with local partners who can ensure an on-going, sustainable push for diversity in their countries' boardrooms. In many of our projects, we partner with WomenCorporateDirectors."

› **Can you share some more examples of recent IFC/WCD initiatives?**

"Sure, there have been several.

"We worked with the Indonesia Chapter of WomenCorporateDirectors and the University of Indonesia to host the country's first roundtable discussion on the role of women on boards. The event addressed the cultural, social, and economic burdens preventing women from reaching the boardroom, and is the first in a planned series of awareness-raising and capacity-building initiatives.

"In Vietnam, we've supported the formation of two WCD chapters, one in Hanoi and one in Ho Chi Minh City. We also helped organize a workshop on board effectiveness for women directors of banks and partnered with WCD in Europe. IFC has also co-sponsored launches of WCD chapters in South Africa, Nigeria, Kenya, and Vietnam. And we've hosted OnBoard Bootcamp training in Singapore and Mumbai.

"In the future, we'll continue to work with WCD to promote diversity on boards — we share an understanding of its importance to organizations all over the world."

WHO SHOULD BE ON A BOARD?

"Nothing is pleasant that is not spiced with variety."

– Francis Bacon

About half of the Fortune 100 companies seek out CEOs or retired CEOs to serve as board directors, and 25 percent of Fortune 100 boards seek out CFOs or retired CFOs. But in today's fast-changing world, the CEO-only model for serving on boards is limiting. After all, many of the best baseball players never make it to the World Series. Many executives who are slightly lower on the corporate totem pole are eminently qualified to sit on a board and could provide much needed skills.

While speaking at the 2nd annual WCD Global Institute, Denise Morrison recalled her own experience: "When I was a general manager at Kraft, I pounded the pavement, trying to get recruiters in New York City to help me get on a board. Doors were shut in my face. I was told, 'You can't be on a board unless you're a sitting CEO.' At that time, there were only four women CEOs in the Fortune 500!

"I didn't understand why somebody like me — who was running a billion dollar business for Kraft and had full P&L accountability — wasn't valued for what I could contribute at the board table. Today, while there is still much to be done, boards are really looking at the skills and competencies needed to move a company in the direction of profitable growth. The *right* people are the ones who take a company to the next level of success."

Good candidates can also come from outside the traditional C-suite. Boards looking for candidates with a fresh point of view should consider someone who's served as president of a university, held a leadership position within the federal government, or worked as an entrepreneur in a privately-owned company. These types of people bring richness to a board, and these types of places are good recruiting grounds for directors.

WCD is working to replace the "entitlement" culture of CEOs on boards with a new multi-gender, multi-national, multi-ethnic, and multi-generational paradigm. In 2012, the organization addressed the challenge by launching the Global Nominating Commission, a high-level task force of board nominating chairs and committee members, as well as CEOs.

Maggie Wilderotter, Chairman and CEO of Frontier Communications Corporation, a director of Xerox Corporation and Procter & Gamble and co-chair of the WCD Global Nominating Commission, describes the commission's mission: "We think of our work in terms of a supply chain, and our mission as ensuring that nominating committees have a ready pool of great candidates for every type of board. By streamlining the nominating process, we speed the time it takes to get a great director on a board, which makes it easier to nominate the next candidate."

While developing a road map of best practices for nominating committees, the commission is taking steps to break down the structural, cultural, and strategic obstacles to change. For example, committees are being encouraged to add diversity (not just in gender, but also in ethnicity, geography, skills sets, and industry backgrounds) to their criteria for evaluating a board candidate. The commission also applauds board term limits so that spots can open up for new and likely diverse directors. As the reality of diversity in the boardroom reaches a critical mass, companies in the lead will find themselves at a distinct advantage over their peers.

"The 20th century was a good time for like-minded people to direct the world, but that's become a liability. In the 21st century, we need boards that inspire organizations to explore different ways of reaching decisions, of understanding disruptions, engaging with uncertainty and resolving crises. Diversity is no longer negotiable; it is essential to thrive and tap into new growth prospects and opportunities. Boards can no longer afford to make assumptions about markets they know nothing about; they must tap into people who bring different perspectives from diverse parts of the world."

Wendy Luhabe | Chairman of Women Private Equity Fund and a director of BMW South Africa, International Management Development in Switzerland, and Abraaj Group in Dubai

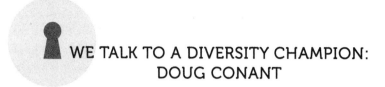

WE TALK TO A DIVERSITY CHAMPION: DOUG CONANT

Doug Conant, Chairman of Avon Products, Founder and CEO of ConantLeadership, Chairman of Kellogg Executive Leadership Institute of Northwestern University and former President and CEO of Campbell Soup Company, is dedicated to helping improve the quality of leadership in the 21st century.

› Why is diversity on boards important?

"It seems to me that one of the most important roles of a board is to help set the cultural tone for the enterprise. In that regard, I think boards need to 'lead from in front' on key dimensions of 'tone setting.' At a minimum, boards certainly should not lag the enterprise on those key dimensions. In my experience, broadly speaking, there are three key dimensions which need to be considered: competence, character, and chemistry.

"In terms of competence, the board must make sure that collectively the board is comprised of people who have the business acumen necessary to guide the enterprise in a successful fashion. In terms of character, the board must make sure that the integrity of all of the directors is beyond reproach. In terms of chemistry, at a minimum, the board must make sure that the 'make up' of the board is responsibly reflective of all of the stakeholders of the enterprise- employees, customers, consumers, investors, regulators, and beyond. Given that half the workforce is made up of women, most enterprises across all stakeholder groups have a meaningful contingent of women stakeholders who arguably, and increasingly, need to feel represented in the boardroom. In my opinion, in order for a board to feel that it has the moral authority to set the tone for the enterprise, it must build itself in a way that honors the need for a highly competent set of directors who are of high character and responsibly diverse.

"Compromising on any one of these three key dimensions should be viewed as unacceptable."

› How did you increase diversity on the board of Campbell Soup Company?

"To begin with, as CEO, my first responsibility was to insure that our management ranks were stocked with a team characterized by high competence, high character, and responsible diversity. We addressed all three key dimensions simultaneously.

"In terms of diversity, given that our products were in virtually every American household with over 80 percent of our consumers being women and over half of our workforce being women, partnering with Catalyst, we built a plan to smartly increase the presence of high competence/high character women at all levels in the organization to a level more consistent with our consumer and employee bases. We advanced those intentions nicely over my decade as CEO, winning the Catalyst Award for our efforts in 2010.

"To the credit of our board, the board clearly felt the need to help 'lead from in front' on this dimension and made diversity a high priority in both board and management succession planning. As a result, we developed a more diverse board and my successor as CEO was a women from our management team, Denise Morrison, the first woman to be CEO of Campbell Soup Company in the over 140 year history of the enterprise. Encouragingly, the company continues to fully embrace diversity under Denise's leadership and continues to maintain a superior total shareowner return profile."

› Do you have advice for other male CEOs/directors about how to increase diversity?

"First, when building a board with the goal of having the moral authority to govern the enterprise, there can be no compromising on candidates. They must all be highly competent, of high character and, in my opinion, appropriately representative of the diversity of the stakeholder base. In my experience, there are plenty of qualified women on all three dimensions.

"Second, the most effective and efficient way to make progress on diversity is to focus on one board slot at a time. Boards are relatively small and intimate communities of executives who are trying to govern an enterprise responsibly. If a board focuses on filling one slot with a fully qualified woman, the progress will be palpable. I cannot imagine a board that does not have the capacity to fill one slot in this manner.

"Third and finally, years ago a friend asked me how I would feel if my daughter was not given a fair opportunity to contribute to the success of an enterprise, be it a sports team, a school, or a work environment. As I reflected on my answer, I became increasingly grounded in the belief that she deserved every opportunity to participate, assuming she was fully qualified. I began to view the world differently after that conversation, as I thought of all the more-than-qualified 'daughters' who were trying to find their way through the challenging world of work.

"The more I leaned into the championing of equal opportunity, I also found that it was in the self-interest of organizations to search out and advance capable women, as those organizations seemed to prosper and perform at a higher level when they fully leveraged the diversity of their resource base.

"Today, at the age of 26, my daughter is the executive director of a highly respected non-profit organization. In her father's humble opinion, she deserved the opportunity and the organization is benefiting from her presence. I encourage male leaders to take the challenge of advancing diversity in a deeply personal way."

WOMEN BREAK THE GRIP OF "GROUP THINK"

"Where all think alike, no one thinks very much."

– Walter Lippmann

When it comes to being a successful board director, it really is the thought that counts.

In the boardroom, companies need brain power, not just big titles. A diversity of ideas enables a company to address and resolve the complex problems facing businesses in an interdependent and unpredictable world. Boards must seek qualified people with different ways of seeing the enterprise and its role. Different points of view give rise to new questions not imagined before. Women champion tough issues because they want to make a difference; they ask more questions and encourage more opinions.

In the WCD/Groysberg/Heidrick & Struggles *2012 Board of Directors Survey*, respondents were asked whether women bring special attributes to the role. Ninety percent of the female directors thought they did, but only 56 percent of the male directors agreed. Specifically:

- 34 percent of women and 57 percent of men said that women bring fresh perspectives and diversity of thought
- 29 percent of women and three percent of men said that women are more willing to ask questions and challenge the status quo
- 20 percent of women and three percent of men said that women are more collaborative and inclusive
- Eight percent of women and 11 percent of men said that women have greater empathy and interpersonal skills

The Société Générale Group report, "Getting the Right Women on Board: Cherchez la Femme," makes the case for women directors, arguing against the "male, pale, and stale" status quo: "More gender-balanced boards can help prevent 'group-think' by introducing new perspectives and experience." A Canadian study by David A.H. Brown, Debra L. Brown and Vanessa Anastasopoulos from the The Conference Board of Canada entitled "Not just the right thing, but the bright thing," found that gender-balanced boards were more likely to identify conflicts of interest and adhere to a code of conduct.

WHAT SKILLS DO WOMEN BRING TO THE BOARDROOM?

Members of WomenCorporateDirectors answer the question:

"In today's boardroom, collaboration skills are very important. Listening skills are very important. Mediating skills are very important. It's these skills that allow you to pull the best from everyone in the room. Once I sat on a board for a technology company where the men had a very aggressive, combative style of dealing with each other. They liked each other, but they really went at it. During my first meeting, I sat there without saying a word. Gradually, I realized what was happening: they all talked, but no one listened. So, I did. Then, I would summarize what had been said and bring out the good points in the yelling. By mediating, I BELIEVED I moved the conversation forward."

– **Judi North**, a director of Acuity Brands, Community Health Systems, and Lumos Networks, co-chair of WCD Atlanta Chapter and an advisory board member of WCD

"Women create an environment in which it's easier to have difficult conversations. We can break the ice, and then keep the conversation going with good manners. Being polite matters if things go south. When it comes to substance, women have different points of view and our perspectives are important. Also, I often see women resolving arguments by asking: 'So, what is the conclusion of this discussion?' What's the action we can take?' I think we make a board more efficient!"

– **Yolanda Auza**, an entrepreneur of Librerias Wilborada 1047, advisory board member of Engineering School Universidad de los Andes and WCD, and co-chair of WCD Colombia Chapter

"While I hate to generalize or stereotype, I'd say women have a higher EQ or Emotional Quotient than men, and that makes them better at consensus building. I think we watch group dynamics closely, and I absolutely believe that women often think differently. All that means is that women can pull a board out of a rut."

– **Sherry Barrat**, retired Vice Chairman of Northern Trust Corporation, a director of NextEra Energy, Inc., Prudential Insurance Funds and Arthur J. Gallagher & Co., and an advisory board member of WCD

"Diversity increases innovation. The more different perspectives you have for decision making, the more creativity you'll get. If members are of the same gender, socio-economic level, or even age, they'll all see things the same way. Diversity in every form improves the conversation."

– **Cathy Allen**, Chairman and CEO of The Santa Fe Group, a director of El Paso Electric Company and Synovus, an advisory board member of WCD, appointed by President Obama to the Valles Caldera Trust Board and co-chair of WCD Greater New Mexico Chapter

CHANGE IS HAPPENING, BUT AT A SNAIL'S PACE

"It takes time to persuade men to do even what is for their own good."

— Thomas Jefferson

Sometimes, boardrooms seem like clubhouses built by 10-year-old boys with the obvious sign hanging on the front door: Girls Keep Out. The *2013 Catalyst Census: Fortune 500 Women Board Directors* reports that women's share of board positions increased only slightly since 2012. Specifically:

In 2012, women held 16.6 percent of board seats at Fortune 500 companies. In 2013, that number bumped up to 16.9 percent. This makes 2013 the eighth consecutive year of virtually no growth in female representation on Fortune 500 boards.

In both 2012 and 2013, less than one-fifth of companies had 25 percent or more women directors, while one-tenth had no women serving on their boards.

Less than one-fourth of companies had three or more women directors serving together in both 2012 (23.1 percent) and 2013 (23.4 percent).

Data from the WCD/Groysberg/Heidrick & Struggles *2012 Board of Directors Survey* suggests that diversity is not a priority for corporate boards: "Boards continue to struggle with diversity … 46 percent of US directors and 57 percent of directors outside the US could not say that seating a diverse representation was priority … Less than half (47 percent/US and 35 percent/non-US) could say their boards had adopted measures that successfully advanced diversity in their boardrooms."

Boris Groysberg, PhD and Deborah Bell, both of Harvard Business School, drive the point home in their article, "Dysfunction in the Boardroom" featured in the *Harvard Business Review*:

"Many people have no doubt that women account for more than 16.6 percent of the pool of highly qualified potential directors, so the question remains: Why aren't more women on boards? One female director offered this explanation: 'Women are not thought of first as candidates unless a board is looking for gender diversity specifically.' Another shared her experience: 'I'm not part of the old boys' network. Directorships go to people who are known. I've been so busy leading my company and raising my family that I'm less well known.' And a third lamented, 'Boards still prefer pale, stale, and male'."

In her article, "The 'Terrible Truth' About Women on Corporate Boards" published in *Forbes*, Judy B. Rosener, a professor at University of California Irvine's Paul Merage School of Business, notes the disparity between what is and what could be: "It's no secret that the number of women on corporate boards in the US has not increased greatly over the last decade … It's no secret that in the US, more women than men now graduate from college. It's no secret that women constitute the largest consumer base in many organizations. It's also no secret that … women tend to ask different kinds of questions than do men; women tend to be more inclusive and collaborative than men; women tend to be more comfortable with ambiguity than men and are more holistic in their thinking …they are different — and tend to bring what can be termed 'added value' to a corporate board."

Groysberg and Bell suggest reasons why progress in getting women "on board" is so very slow:

1) Women and men disagree on the "whose job is it" question.
A large majority of women say that the task of building a diverse corporate board falls to board leadership. "Women view the board chairs, lead directors, and nominating committee chairs as the real change agents in building a diverse boardroom," says Henrietta Fore, Chairman and CEO of Holsman International, co-chair of the Asia Society, a director of Exxon Mobil Corporation, Aspen Institute, General Mills, Theravance Biopharma, Inc., Seaward International Company, Committee for Economic Development, and Stockton Products, and an advisory board member and global co-chair of WCD. Men, on the other hand, think that it's more important to develop a pipeline of diverse board candidates through director advocacy, mentorship, and training.

2) Men and women differ on the reason why women are under-represented on boards.
Men (45 percent) believe that the "lack of women in executive ranks" is the primary reason that the percentage of women on boards remains low. Women (35 percent) say it because "traditional networks tend to be male-oriented." This suggests that

female directors think women need access to the kinds of networks that men have historically enjoyed if they hope to make gains in the boardroom.

3) Many boards don't know best practices in this area; they simply don't know how to proceed.

Worldwide, boards are facing both a "push" and "pull" toward increasing diversity, resulting in a heightened call to address the issue and a lot of different solutions for getting the job done. While the percentage of board seats held by women varies country by country, there is no getting around the hard fact: women's representation on boards comes nowhere close to parity.

Are there pockets of progress?

In a study, Credit Suisse AG Research Institute interviewed 2,360 companies to answer the question: "Does gender diversity within corporate management improve performance?" The study included these stage-setting observations:

- Companies in industries closer to final consumer demand — for example, retail, healthcare, and finance — have more women on their boards. Conversely (and not surprisingly), heavy industry and information technology companies have a much lower proportion of women board members, with 50 percent of these types having none at all.
- Companies in Europe have relatively high ratios of women on the board, which makes perfect sense given the introduction of quotas, both mandatory and voluntary, in several EU countries (read more on page 53). In contrast, among Asian companies, 72 percent have no women directors (among North American companies, only 16 percent have none). Also, in Asia and Latin America, the number of companies with three or more women on the board is insignificant.
- Larger companies are much more likely to have women on the board than smaller companies. Generally, the greater the number of employees, the larger the talent pool. As the researchers note:
    - "On average, it is the large cap and higher profile companies that have added women at senior management levels...
    - "On average, companies with three or more women on the board have

a market capitalization three times greater than that of companies with no women board members."

At the same time, in their article in *Directors & Boards* "Boards and the permanent revolution in governance," Theodore Dysart, Vice Chairman of Heidrick & Struggles and a leader in the global Board of Directors Practice and Bonnie Gwin, Vice Chairman and Managing Partner of North America Board of Directors Practice of Heidrick & Struggles and a director of Georgetown University Board of Regents argue that: "External pressure to achieve diversity on boards will continue to come from a broad array of sources: advocacy groups, corporate governance watchdogs, and institutional investors, including pension funds, labor unions, the government, and sustainable investment firms ... In recent years, boards have done a good job of shedding dysfunctional directors — those members who are completely disengaged or, at the opposite end, disruptive and obstructionist to no purpose. But many boards have been less inclined to deal with a more insidious phenomena in their midst — the 'go-along-get along' underperformer who makes no waves but also adds little value. Such reluctance infuriates investors, and the increasingly complex world in which companies must operate will compel boards to address those weak links."

"A woman can spend many, many years trying to break the glass ceiling and, when she does, she often finds a culture and agenda created for men by men. It is often an intense and exclusive culture and not the best environment for women to thrive in. It is the same in the board room- so as we get more women on boards and want them to be effective and stay- we need to change the culture in the meeting room as well."

Pernille Spiers-Lopez | former President of IKEA US and a director of Coop, Dk and Meijer, Inc.

YES, THERE'S A BUSINESS CASE FOR DIVERSITY

"What's dangerous is not to evolve."

— Jeff Bezos

Diversity makes good business sense. Just as nations thrive when they develop inclusive political and economic institutions (and fail when power is in the hands of only a few), businesses do better when diverse perspectives lead to better choices. Of course, diversity doesn't "just happen": it requires innovative leadership, corporate transparency, and openness to new ideas.

In the report, "Fulfilling the Promise: How More Women on Corporate Boards Would Make America and American Companies More Competitive," the Committee for Economic Development doesn't pull any punches: "We have one fundamental recommendation: Businesses —business leaders — must make it a priority to develop the talents and advance the careers of female staff who have been identified as potential leaders. This means providing such women with the experiences and backgrounds needed to rise to the top, and advocating their promotion to higher levels of responsibility. The development of talent within an organization is critical to long-term competitiveness."

Annual studies by Catalyst, an organization that promotes women in the workplace, and McKinsey Consulting have shown that companies with more women directors rank higher on various performance measures. Specifically, companies with the highest percentages of women board directors have realized more than 50 percent higher return on equity, more than 40 percent higher return on sales, and more than 65 percent higher return on invested capital. In the recent book *Why Diversity Matters*, Catalyst concludes that the business case for diversity has four dimensions: financial performance, talent management, reputation, and innovation.

In the United Kingdom, the Davies Report "Women on Boards" says that "corporate boards perform better when they include the best people who come from a range of perspectives and backgrounds ... No company will remain competitive for long if it ignores half of its available labor pool." Other studies contend that companies with women on their boards do a better job of engaging with society and customers, which improves the public trust and shareholder value.

"Putting women on the board isn't about 'feeling good' or 'doing good'. It's absolutely great for business."

the late **Fritzi Woods** | a former director of Jamba Juice and Ignite Restaurants

SEVEN REASONS WHY GREATER GENDER DIVERSITY MEANS BETTER CORPORATE PERFORMANCE

From "Gender Diversity and Corporate Performance,"
Credit Suisse Research

A signal of a better company. Having women on the board sends a "positive signal" to the market — a signal that the company has a "greater focus on corporate governance" or that it is doing well since "it is mostly the larger companies that ... have already performed well, which are more likely to appoint female board representatives."

Greater effort across the board. In studies of team dynamics, Katherine Phillips, the senior vice dean of Columbia Business School, has found that: (a) individuals are likely to prepare more for an exercise that will involve working with a diverse, rather than a homogenous, group; (b) a wider range of inputs are likely to be debated in a diverse rather than a homogenous setting; and (c) a diverse group, in the end, is more likely to generate the correct answer to a particular problem than will a homogenous group.

A better mix of leadership skills. In its report, "Women Matter 2: Female leadership, a competitive edge for the future," McKinsey highlighted the differences in male and female leadership styles. " ... there are nine key criteria that, on average, define any good leader. Interestingly, women apply five of these nine leadership behaviors more frequently than men. For instance, women were found to be particularly good at defining responsibilities clearly ... "

Access to a wider pool of talent. Across most markets, women now account for the greater proportion of graduates—54 percent, up from 51 percent in 2000, according to UNESCO. Companies committed to gender diversity tap into the widest possible pool of talent.

A better reflection of the consumer. If, as studies show, women are more likely to be responsible for household spending decisions, then a corporate board with female representation could better understand customer preferences. Consumer-facing industries already rank among those with the greater proportion of women on the board. Industrial companies rank among the lowest.

Improved corporate governance. Many studies show that companies with three or more women on their boards perform better, not just financially, but in governance, including communicating with employees, prioritizing customer satisfaction, and considering corporate social responsibility.

Risk aversion. The research of Nick Wilson, Professor of Credit Management at Leeds University Business School, shows that having at least one female director on the board appears to reduce a company's likelihood of becoming bankrupt by 20 percent, and that having two or three lowers the likelihood even more.

UNDER DEBATE: QUOTAS AND TERM LIMITS/MANDATORY RETIREMENT

"Standing in the middle of the road is very dangerous; you get knocked down by the traffic from both sides."

— Margaret Thatcher

After the "what" and "why" of diversity comes the "how": Are there mechanisms that work successfully to make diversity more likely or even commonplace? Debate is lively around two possibilities: quotas and term limits/mandatory retirement. But there's still no agreement about either one's fairness or effectiveness.

Quotas

The majority by a wide margin (77 percent) of the directors who participated in the WCD/Heidrick & Struggles *2013 Board of Directors Survey* said that their boards do not have a quota or diversity target. However, 71 percent of directors at African companies and 48 percent of directors at European companies report having a quota or target. In Asia, 16 percent report diversity targets, while in North America the figure is only three percent.

Among the directors who reported a target or quota, 60 percent felt that it has strengthened the board. But that opinion was split by gender, with 74 percent of female directors saying the targets were a positive, but only about 50 percent of men saying the same. In their research surrounding the WCD/Groysberg/Heidrick & Struggles *2012 Board of Directors Survey*, Boris Groysberg, PhD and Deborah Bell found that men in countries with quotas support them in higher numbers than do men in countries without them (43 percent versus 23 percent), while nearly all women directors in countries with quotas say they are effective (95 percent).

Alison Winter, CEO of Braintree Holdings LLC, Co-founder and an advisory board member of WCD and a director of Nordstrom, Inc. and Blain's Supply, likens quotas to affirmative action: "Was affirmative action necessary? Yes. We would not have had greater diversity, as quickly, whether by gender or race, if there hadn't been affirmative action. So, I think setting targets creates movement in the right direction."

But Pat McKay, a Partner and Managing Director of Templeton & Company LLP, a trustee of Committee for Economic Development, an advisory board member and CFO of WCD and co-chair of WCD South Florida Chapter, argues against them: "The potential downside of a quota is that a board might fill a position with a woman who's not appropriate for the job, and that would be detrimental. If diversity is voluntary, we'll find better receptivity and we'll end up with a much better result. Of course, every board wants great candidates, so 'diversity' *per se* is not the point because gender is not what makes a director 'great.' Nonetheless, we need to figure out how to get more 'great' women in front of boards for their consideration."

WHAT'S HAPPENING AROUND THE WORLD?

In its report, "Getting the Right Women on Board: Cherchez la Femme," The Société Générale Group provides these summaries of global activities, including the relative success of quotas, by country:

Norway is the most aggressive, with a 40 percent target for public companies. The quotas include heavy sanctions, the toughest of which is the forced dissolution of non-compliant companies.

Spain's 2007 law on Effective Equality between Women and Men recommended that companies with more than 250 employees gradually appoint women on their boards until a proportion of at least 40/60 was reached by 2015. Companies reaching this quota will be given priority status in the allocation of government contracts. There are no formal sanctions. Progress has been limited.

France has experienced one of the most rapid increases in women board members, jumping from 12.3 percent in 2008 to 22.3 percent in 2012. Companies with at least 500 employees and revenues over €50 million are obliged to appoint at least 20 percent women on their boards within three years (2015), and 40 percent within six years. The sanctions for non-compliance are the voiding of nominations and the suspension of fees to all board members.

The Netherlands adopted a legal target of at least 30 percent representation for each gender by January 2016, applicable to both listed and non-listed companies with more than 250 employees. The Dutch are unique in requiring women on both the management and supervisory boards.

Italy introduced quotas of at least one-third of each gender on boards of listed and state-owned companies by 2015. Sanctions begin with a warning, followed by fines, and ultimately forfeiture of the offices of all members of the board. But from 2008 to 2011, representation has only risen from 3.2 percent to 4.4 percent; in 2011 more than 50 percent of companies still had no women.

In Belgium, the boards of publicly-listed companies must have at least one-third of each gender, state companies have one year to comply, listed companies have six years, and small to medium-sized listed firms have eight years. Sanctions for noncompliance are the loss of benefits by board members until compliance. If the quota has still not been reached one year later, a new board will be appointed.

Companies in Asia and the Middle East have far fewer women in their boards, with Saudi Arabia and Qatar at the bottom at .1 percent and .3 percent respectively. Japan is also lagging global trends, with only .9 percent of its directors being women.

Where diversity is voluntary — Austria, Belgium, Denmark, Finland, France, Germany, Luxembourg, the Netherlands, Poland, Spain, and Sweden — progress follows peer pressure and demands from stakeholders and the media. In Sweden and Finland, about one in four board members are women (27 percent and 26 percent, respectively). In the United Kingdom, the government is working to develop business-led initiatives promoting women on boards. A review led by Lord Davies recommended that listed companies have at least 25 percent female board members by 2015.

WOMEN ON BOARDS IN THE MIDDLE EAST:
PRIVATE SECTOR MOVING DIVERSITY FORWARD

Two women from the Middle East spoke at the third annual WCD Global Institute which convened more than 250 board directors from both the corporate and nonprofit sectors around the world: Fatima Al Jaber of the United Arab Emirates, a director and the Head of Projects Committee of Al Jaber Group, Chairperson of Al Bashayer Investment Company PJSC, Abu Dhabi Businesswomen's Council and UAE Businesswomen's Council, a director of Abu Dhabi Chamber of Commerce and Industry and Abu Dhabi Council for Economic Development, and chair of the WCD Gulf Cooperation Council Chapter, and Fatin Yousef Bundagji, President of the TLC Management & Development Consultancy and a director of the Jeddah Chamber of Commerce and Industry.

Fatima Al Jaber and Fatin Yousel Bundagi addressed the question: How are women directors driving corporate governance and diversity in the region?

"Saudi women are gradually trailblazing their way into positions of authority through their 'voice' and 'presence.' They are vocalizing the need for reform by calling for more openness, transparency, and good governance at all levels of management: public, private and civil. It seems that this newfound power is the result of their actual powerlessness; simply put, they have nothing to lose but lots to gain." says Bundagji, who is also a founding member of the Baladi Campaign, a civil society initiative aiming to mobilize the political participation of women in Saudi Arabia. Al Jaber contends that diversity is giving private companies in the UAE "better decision-making, better transparency, and more governance in the decision-making criteria."

The change agents for reform are women.

Bundagji supports quotas to increase diversity on corporate boards: "For now, and until such a time when diversity on boards becomes the norm, we have to have a quota system in place for women's inclusion. We cannot wait for equality to happen; there are generations of young adults in waiting, who have lost all patience and who are demanding to take their rightful place in our world... Saudi Arabia has been mastering the concept of resiliency ever since its creation." Al Jaber argues that one strategy to grow the number of women on boards depends on female directors themselves: "We, as women, share a responsibility to promote ourselves and each other for director positions."

Both agree that reaching out to individuals, one-on-one, is necessary to propel women to board positions and to advance their leadership. As Bundagji argues: "Individual-to-individual interaction or citizen-to-citizen diplomacy is key to advancing this cause as it helps change attitudes and mindsets and promotes buy-in."

In March 2013, WCD launched its first Middle East chapter in the Gulf Cooperation Council in Abu Dhabi.

TERM LIMITS/MANDATORY RETIREMENT

The *Wall Street Journal* reported that the average tenure of directors among companies in the S&P 1500 index hit a record high of 10.8 years in 2013, according to Institutional Shareholder Services. That's up from 8.7 in 2007. Other research suggests that most boards average one member rotating off every two years — a glacial pace, unless one's board construct is perfect.

The Spencer Stuart and Corporate Board Member report "What Directors Think" — a survey of directors at S&P 500 companies —says that retirement ages are being pushed back, and as a result, "board members are becoming older and more entrenched." Just over half (53 percent) of the survey participants said that their boards have a mandatory retirement age.

When asked whether it would create a problem for a director to serve as much as 30 years on one board, respondents were split, with 53 percent saying yes and 47 percent saying no. The report's authors, Deborah Scally and Kimberly Crowe, quote one survey respondent who articulated the ambivalence around term limits and mandatory retirement: "I generally favor age limits, but [Warren] Buffett is causing me to rethink the issue. Who wouldn't want Buffett at 80-plus?" Another pointed out that proponents for age limits "seem to focus on the negative side of longevity but give little or no credence to the wisdom gained only through years of experience."

The WCD/Heidrick & Struggles *2013 Board of Directors Survey* reports that term limits are supported by comfortable majorities in every region of the globe except North America, where the figure is a little over 40 percent, compared to Central and South America (74 percent), Africa (71 percent), Europe (70 percent), Australia (63 percent), and Asia (63 percent). Globally, male and female directors support term limits in about equal numbers, 53 percent and 56 percent, respectively. Among the directors participating in the survey: 52 percent of men and 48 percent of women said they support mandatory retirement, and 65 percent of these supporters put the ideal age between 70 and 74. Yet, several respondents said that their boards waive mandatory retirement when they want to keep a director longer.

IS THREE THE MAGIC NUMBER?

"When an idea reaches critical mass there is no stopping the shift its presence will induce."

– Marianne Williamson

James Kristie, Editor and Associate publisher of *Directors & Boards* and an advisory board member of the Center for Corporate Governance of Drexel University, says, "One woman on a board is a token; two is a presence; three is a voice." At WCD, we say that in effect, "One woman is invisible; two are a conspiracy; three are mainstream." Anecdotal evidence and qualitative research agree that three women on a board is the minimum number for achieving positive, meaningful results.

"I'm a strong believer that diversity generates innovation and 'out of the box' thinking," says Cathy Allen. "When I'm on a board and there are two women, I work very hard to get the third because I think that's the tipping point in performance. And performance is the most important thing."

When the Société Générale Group investigated the relationship between the percentage of women on companies' boards and their share price performance, the result was clear: when representation is 30 percent or more, a company outperforms those with fewer women on their boards. The report from McKinsey reached the same conclusion: performance increases significantly once a critical mass of 30 percent of women at board level is attained.

In her study of 11 Israeli companies who have had gender-balanced boards for two decades, Miriam Schwartz Ziv, an assistant professor of Finance at Michigan State University, found that in meetings, boards with at least three directors of each gender in attendance were approximately twice as likely both to request further information and to take an initiative, compared to boards without gender balance. In fact, everyone — men and women alike — were more active when at least three women directors were in attendance. Also, these companies had significantly greater return on equity and net profit margin.

Merle Okawara, a former director of Avon Products (Japan), Chairman of JC Comsa Corporation, a director of Parco and co-chair of WCD Japan Chapter, is sure that having three women "on board" makes a difference in the quality of the conversation and in decision making: "I advocate for quotas in Japan because otherwise we won't get at least three women on every board. You have to understand, in Japan, when you write the character for 'woman' three times, it spells 'cacophony' or 'disaster.' When a woman is alone on a board, without support, it's hard to make a point; the men look the other way or they don't listen. But three women make a critical mass. It's easier to explain your thoughts, ideas, and decisions without seeming too forward."

"When you're the only woman on a board, you feel like the exception to the rule. How often have you been in a meeting and watched a woman speak up, only to be ignored, and then a man says the same thing a few minutes later and is credited with a great idea? When you have two or three women at the table, you can watch for these behaviors and call them out. Funny, when you do, the men usually appreciate it. They don't realize that they're often dismissing the woman in the room."

Sherry Barrat | retired Vice Chairman of Northern Trust Corporation, a director of NextEra Energy, Inc., Prudential Insurance Funds and Arthur J. Gallagher & Co., and an advisory board member of WCD

"THE POWER OF THREE"

Several successful women address the question of representation in the article entitled "The Power of Three: Three Women on a Board" published in *Directors & Boards*. Here are excerpts of their discussion:

Maggie Wilderotter, Chairman and CEO of Frontier Communications Corporation, a director at Xerox Corporation, and Proctor & Gamble and co-chair of the WCD Global Nominating Commission

"I have sat on 23 public company boards in my career. Except for two, I have always been the first woman to join the board ... Breaking the ice to getting more women on a board [begins with] the first woman ... Then you can prove to the other board members that we are not scary and that we can actually add to the conversation and to making good decisions. The board then develops a level of comfort that having different opinions in the room is okay.

"A great example is when I joined the Yahoo! Inc. board. That was four years ago, and I was the first woman on the board. Silicon Valley boards are typically venture capitalists — it is still a 'boys club' environment for many tech boards — so the Yahoo! board was taking a chance, and so was I. I gave them a level of comfort that having a woman was okay and that more women could be added to the board ... [Still] it is not a foregone conclusion that one woman can't make an impact and that you must have multiple women on the board to make a difference. I have been on boards with one or two women who have had a very strong voice on those boards and were not taken for granted. And I have been on a board with three women where that was not necessarily the case.

"What really matters is the leadership of the board, the culture of the board, and the capabilities of the women and men who serve on those boards."

Lulu Wang, a director of MetLife Insurance Company and Asia Society, Overseer of Columbia Business School, an advisory council member of U.S. Trust, and an advisory board member of WCD

"… women do their homework. They read the materials. When you do that, you are in better position to ask questions. Then you're not afraid to ask a 'dumb question' … Often a board discussion will involve a matter that is perplexing to me. Just as the discussion is about to move on and I am deciding whether to ask a question, I hear another woman director's voice say, 'This may be a small point but can you just clarify it for me?' Having it clarified helps illuminate the whole discussion for all the board members. Women are good at this — having the willingness to ask a question because they have done the reading.

"The role of the board is to understand the complex issues of the business that we are engaged in — the big picture as well as the long-term picture. Very often I find my fellow women board members will, in the heat of a discussion — perhaps in making an acquisition — say, 'Hold it a second. Let's just step back a bit. How does this fit into our long-term strategic plan here? How does this acquisition really position us? Is it taking us off the track of what we've been talking about as our long-term positioning?' That stepping back and looking at the forest and not the trees is such an important part of what a board does, and I think that women do it very well.

"I was involved in a board situation where I was the first woman to be on the investment committee in its 50-year history. The committee chair was a crusty 70-year-old guy who didn't know that women could do anything in the investment world. In the beginning, I was the invisible woman. Whenever the discussion went around the table, he never quite got to asking me my opinion. I didn't take offense, because I knew that he really didn't understand that I existed. But then it became time for me to earn my stripes. I made a point of having an opinion on everything. This was probably a nuisance to him at first, but within the year he began to want to hear my voice. I have been on that committee for about 10 years now and, as he is getting ready to retire from his chairmanship, he paid me a great compliment. He said, 'Lulu, you are the one voice I really want to hear on this committee.' It took him a long time, but during that time the staff watched me go from being the invisible woman to the woman whose voice was heard — who made it be heard because I persisted — to finally the one voice that the men wanted to hear. That is a lesson we can all take away."

Eileen Kamerick, CFO of Press Ganey Associates, Inc. and a director of Associated Bancorp Westell Technologies, and Legg Mason & Co., LLC

"People think of bank boards as perhaps the most 'clubby' of all boards. For a long time, Associated Banc had no women directors. Interestingly, it was the shareholders at the annual meetings who kept asking the longtime CEO, 'Why don't you have any women on the board?' His response was, 'I can't find any who are qualified' ... There was a fair amount of unrest that this was not an appropriate response. So when a new CEO came in about eight years ago, he sought out women for the board. It was really because of his leadership that there are now three women on the board.

"There can be in some boardrooms a sort of old boys club go-along get-along dynamic. Because women are by their very nature not part of this club, they have an ability to raise topics in a way that people find less threatening and are more willing to be open about. I experienced this in an interesting way on a board with another woman director when a third woman joined us. I respected her enormously, but it seemed like we disagreed on just about every issue. We had entirely different backgrounds and entirely different points of view in every possible way. We were mutually respectful in our disagreements, but by the two of us having that dialogue it opened up topics that people found difficult to deal with. It drove a richness and depth to the discussion."

Donna James, Managing Director of Lardon & Associates, LLC and director of L Brands, Time Warner Cable, Marathon Petroleum Corporation, and FIS Group

"There is an added degree of comfort in seeing another woman across the table, especially when something like this happens: A woman will put an issue on the table, and then one of the men will say the exact same thing. It sounds like something different has been said when it really hasn't. Your female colleague can catch that when it happens and flip the script of the conversation by saying, 'Yes, that's Donna's point.' I don't want to detract from my male colleagues, who are capable of vigorous and good discussion. But it does something for your own psyche, personally and professionally, to hear multiple female voices making points that are meaningful and substantive."

Kyung H. Yoon, Founder and CEO of Talent Age Associates, Co-founder and Partner of Executive Board Exchange, a director of MCM Worldwide/Sungjoo Group, and former Chairman and President of Asia America MultiTechnology Association

"When I came on the Silicon Valley Bank board I was the second woman … I came on to contribute my expertise to talent and organizational development and the bank's expansion into Asia. Two more women have since joined the board — one is an entrepreneur and financial investor and the other is a venture capitalist. So one after another, each of us brought something else to the table. Given the bank's expansion and its focus on globalization and doing business in innovative ways, the women have added a lot to the conversation. We're not only looking at creative new ways of doing things; we're also ensuring sensitivity to the impact of the bank's actions on people all around the world.

"I find that women are not 'baked into' relationships. They don't make assumptions about the dynamics of the board. They will raise their hand and say, 'We need to talk about this some more.' Or, 'How about some more facts.' Or, 'Have you thought about this?' Doing that changes the dynamics of things getting done just because that's the way they have always gotten done."

NEW AND DIFFERENT SKILLS ARE IN DEMAND

"Intelligence is the ability to adapt to change."

— Stephen Hawking

Traditionally, financial expertise is the No. 1 skill sought in a director. In 2012, more than 40 percent of directors on corporate boards had once been CFOs in their professional careers, according to Ernst & Young's report "CFO and beyond: The possibilities and pathways outside finance." But the world is changing and, despite anxieties about the global economy, other skills are now being recognized as important. Executives with expertise in global branding, supply chain management, strategic talent, risk management, cyber security, IT (including digital and social media), and manufacturing in emerging markets can make excellent directors.

"Boards are looking for people with good judgment, who have accomplishment, who demonstrate wisdom, and who can focus on strategy and good governance. No one is expected to be an expert in every functional area; it is more important to draw on one's overall experience and knowledge, and to be able to ask the right questions," says Shirley Ann Jackson, PhD, President of Rensselaer Polytechnic Institute, and a director of IBM, FedEx, Marathon Oil, Medtronic, and PSEG.

In fact, the idea of value is evolving, as Pat McKay explains: "When it comes to finding women with 'profit-and-loss responsibility' on their resumes, the demand may be higher than the supply. But that's okay because functional capabilities, especially finance and IT expertise, are also good to have. Ultimately, the soft skills matter — the ability *not* to take a dogmatic approach; the ability to be thoughtful and collaborative — these skills enable women to make a strategic difference to a company."

Jan Babiak recommends global experience: "Boards are really interested in people who have lived and breathed a 'global' career. Sometimes people will claim 'international experience' just because they have some overseas employees reporting to them. But that doesn't carry as much credibility as actually living abroad and experiencing a different economy and culture."

How do women directors think of their own strengths?

According to the WCD/Groysberg/Heidrick & Struggles *2012 Board of Directors Survey*, the top skills women say they bring to the board are industry knowledge, financial/auditing expertise, and strategic ability. Only seven percent believe international/global experience is their strongest skill set. And less than five percent of all the respondents (men and women) rate the following critical skills as their strongest: regulatory, legal and compliance; technology; risk management; compensation; M&A; HR talent management; succession planning; and evaluation-assessment.

Forty-three percent of US directors and 42 percent of non-US directors say specific expertise is missing or insufficiently represented on their boards. US directors say that "technology expertise" is missing or underrepresented; directors outside the United States bemoan a deficiency in "HR/talent management" skill at the board level.

One exercise during OnBoard Bootcamp (a WCD-sponsored seminar for board hopefuls) is a real-world case study of a director search conducted for a global, cement company. Working with one of the authors, management created a Skills Set Matrix to be assured of covering all the bases and to enable a fair apples-to-apples comparison of each candidate (see the sidebar). When you're a board candidate, ask whether such a matrix will be used as part of the interview/evaluation process, and then suggest that you could fill it out yourself. Also, it's a good idea to create your own matrix highlighting your relevant skills and experiences that might not show up on the company's version.

WHAT'S A GOOD SKILL FIT FOR YOU?

Large Board

Strategic skills

Engineering/IT skills

Knowledge of relevant/future markets

Helpful political/alliance/client contacts

Experience in situations facing company

Experience with "same as" or "want to be" companies

Cyber Security

Risk Management

Small Board

Understanding of relevant markets and trends

Key contacts

Experience with finding capital investors

Experience growing a company/taking it public

Generating good PR or references

Experience in hiring/managing/mentoring talent

Source: OnBoard Bootcamp

ACTION TIPS

If you haven't owned a profit and loss division, ask for it. Even if it's a small product line, understanding the process of budgeting, forecasting and driving results is necessary.

Volunteer for the tough roles.

Network and apply for upper management roles. Men apply confidently for positions when they meet about 60 percent of the requirements; women hesitate to apply when they have 100 percent covered according to The Atlantic article "The Confidence Gap" by Katty Kay and Claire Shipman authors of *The Confidence Code: The Science and Art of Self-Assurance—What Women Should Know.*

Volunteer for projects that will give you more leadership visibility.

Grab any opportunity to present at your company's full board or board committees. You'll learn a great deal about the process and protocol, plus you'll be establishing relationships with board members who may help you get placed.

Use an executive coach to help you position yourself effectively.

SKILLS SET MATRIX

Note: All candidates will have energy, intelligence, and integrity

	NAME	NAME	NAME
GENERAL EXPERTISE			
Industry knowledge			X
"Off the grid" thinking		X	X
Top government position	X		
Academic qualifications	X	X	X
US connections	X	X	
Global connections/view		X	X
Diversity	X	X	X
Governance experience	X		
Environment/social responsibility/Sustainable development	X	X	
Corporate and advisory boards			X
Independence	X	X	X
Financial expertise		X	
CORPORATE MANAGEMENT/ ENTREPRENEUR			
Technology/e-commerce/IT		X	
New product development			X
Success in building or adding value to a growing/profitable business	X	X	
Branding/marketing/communications/media			X
Strategic planning	X		
Financial/CFO	X		
Labor management		X	
Sales		X	X
External relations	X	X	X
Government/regulatory and public affairs	X		
Procurement/supply chain/Operations/customer service		X	
Strategic alliances/mergers and Acquisitions		X	
Cyber Security			
Risk Management			

Source: OnBoard Bootcamp

TEN BIG IDEAS ON THE MINDS OF WOMEN CORPORATE DIRECTORS

"Great minds have purposes; others have wishes."

– Washington Irving

As women globally gain more footholds in boardrooms — even as numbers in the U.S. stay constant — they share common priorities in governing their companies and ensuring the survival of their organizations. At WomenCorporateDirectors' third annual Global Institute, more than 250 women corporate directors, board chairs, CEOs, executives, and policy experts discussed and debated topics challenging boards today, from regulation to the growing power of emerging markets.

Here are the top ten:

1. Competition in capital markets: Competitive pressures are tougher than ever in every area, from innovation and pricing to natural resources and consumer mindshare. "Capital markets are the most competitive markets companies have to address. You are competing with every single company in every single industry for that rare resource: equity," according to Marina Brogi, Deputy Dean Faculty of Economics at Sapienza Università di Roma, a director of Salini-Impregilo and Ubi Banca, co-chair of WCD Milan Chapter and an advisory board member of WCD.

2. Moving away from fierce investor short-termism: Relentless investor focus on quarterly earnings can inhibit company growth, a problem that's exacerbated by the way companies have traditionally reported results. "Changing the language about corporate reporting to incorporate the idea of 'integrated reporting' can help raise the visibility and adoption of better corporate social responsibility, more ethical behavior, and greater accountability," says Alison Winter.

3. Entering new markets – carefully: As companies weigh the opportunities and risks of investing in new markets, boards understand that each market requires a thoughtful, tailored approach. What's the best way to go into these countries? A public/private approach? A joint venture with companies already there? How can a company best connect to the local communities?

4. Board education on a global level: When companies evaluate emerging markets, boards are also bringing in experts who can help bring them up to speed on the multiple complex issues that arise. "Our board clients are really taking the time to invite in the emerging markets' leaders from the company management to provide the appropriate level of briefing – whether it's about compliance issues or the supply chain or talent," says Anne Lim O'Brien, Vice Chairman at Heidrick & Struggles. "It's about bringing that expertise into the boardroom and then making this a best practice."

5. Identifying the real risks: Boards are starting to educate themselves about the threats and opportunities posed by big data and the cloud, but the learning curve is steep. "Some companies worry about the security and reliability of cloud computing, but for the vast majority of applications for the vast majority of organizations, moving to the cloud is actually more secure than trying to maintain their own data centers," says Clara Shih, CEO and Founder of Hearsay Social and a director of Starbucks Corporation.

6. Differing pace of technology adoption across the world: Companies are learning that various consumer markets can take very different paths to current technology, as newer markets often leapfrog certain technologies altogether. "Boards need to understand that in emerging markets the first touch point consumers have with the internet is not their computer, but their phone," says Myla Villanueva, CEO of Novare Technologies, Founder and Managing Director of MDI Group Holdings, and co-chair of WCD Philippines Chapter.

7. Building in sustainability: Creating a sustainable enterprise is no longer just about CSR lip service. Companies are developing sustainable practices on firm footing by partnering with their consumers. "Give the consumer the opportunity to be part of sustainable solutions…if we all want to live like Americans, we'll need five planet Earths," contends Paul Polman, CEO and executive director of Unilever,

Chair of the World Business Council of Sustainable Development, and a director of the UN Global Compact Paul and the Dow Chemical Company.

8. Women's consumer power is disrupting business as usual: Women's buying power and influence are forcing companies to rethink their business models. "Disruptive innovation will become the norm, and women are the disruptive technology in the next century," says Usha Rao-Monari, a director and CEO of Global Water Development Partners, a Blackstone Portfolio Company.

9. Impact of more women on boards: "Fitting in" was the old model of women in the boardroom; the new model is that women are changing the rules. "In the boardroom women face the unwritten rules men have unconsciously developed and unconsciously want to protect, and we go into the game and break these rules, just as unconsciously. We cause discomfort and they wish we weren't there," says Susan Oliver, Chair of Scale Investors Ltd, and retired Chair of Fusion Retail Brands.

10. True boardroom equality: As more women move into positions of power in companies, the "woman" identifier will become less important. "Real equality will look like women being put on boards not because of their gender, but because of the quality of their work," concludes Marjorie Scardino, Former CEO of Pearson.

"Have a **bias** toward **action.** You can break that **big plan into** small steps and take the first step right away."

– Indira Gandhi

The boardroom is no place for the shy or hesitant. Getting there requires gumption and planning. How can you become the best pick among worthy contenders? Consider the advice of Confucius: "Instead of being concerned that you are not known, seek to be worthy of being known." This section is about opening doors and preparing for opportunities.

"Getting on a board doesn't happen overnight; it's a career-long pursuit that YOU must orchestrate with deliberate intent toward the ultimate goal. You have to be very visible and build a network of people who already serve on corporate boards so they know who you are. You can't decide to get ready for board work two years before you're going to retire from your day job—there are too many qualified men who are waiting in the wings, as well as other exceptional women who have been preparing for the same opportunity for years."

Betsy Berkhemer-Credaire
President and co-founder of Berkhemer Clayton Retained Executive Search, author of *The Board Game—How Smart Women Become Corporate Directors*
and co-chair of WCD Los Angeles Chapter

GETTING A SEAT AT THE TABLE

WHEN OPPORTUNITY KNOCKS, OPEN THE DOOR

"Ask for what you want and be prepared to get it."

– Maya Angelou

If you're invited to serve on a board, you've got what it takes to contribute to its success. And it's okay to go for the job if you have only 75 percent of the qualifications, as long as you have the confidence that comes from preparation.

"While women build strategic plans for their brands or for their companies, they don't do strategic plans for themselves and their careers. But they should," says Denise Morrison. "Boards are responsible for a company's strategy, for understanding its appetite for risk, and making sure that the right talent is in place, starting with the CEO. Women wanting to be directors should be in the habit of thinking strategically."

KPMG's Kathy Hopinkah Hannan uses similar language in advising women how to prepare for a seat at the table: "You have to have a brand. Should you be more aggressive? Should you be less aggressive? When I hear people say women should 'act like men,' I think that's a waste of time. Women are equal to men. Period. The important thing is to be authentic: If you think you deserve to be in the boardroom, act that way."

The late Fritzi Woods liked to suggest getting practical: "It's never too early to make a plan. Develop a skills set; start building your resume; work on a non-profit board where you can align your purpose and passion, but do that strategically by deciding, in advance, what you want to get out of the experience. If nothing else, find out who else is on that board."

One good place to get ready for board service is a training preparedness program.

For example, OnBoard Bootcamp is a one-day seminar designed for those (a) who are already on a non-profit or small-company board but who would like to join a larger one, (b) who are about to become a board member, (c) who would like to be selected for a board, or (d) who would like to establish an action plan for getting on a board. During OnBoard Bootcamp, experienced corporate directors and search executives share "lessons learned" from an insider's perspective.

According to the coaches at OnBoard Bootcamp, if you can answer "yes" to the following statements, your chances of obtaining a seat at the corporate board table are much better than average.

1. I have identified the corporation on whose board I wish to serve.
2. I am clear as to why I have chosen this corporation.
3. I have spent time researching the company and the industry and I would be proud to serve.
4. I have sent for the corporation's annual report and reviewed the website.
5. I have identified current directors and the industries they represent.
6. I have looked at past proxies, analysts' reports, and press clips.
7. I can name the CEO, CFO, and COO.
8. I have identified what value I can bring to the table.
9. I am committed to allocating the time and preparation required to be an effective board member. The average director spends up to 200 hours each year on board business.
10. I have increased my visibility by getting involved in not-for-profit organizations, events, and projects that I truly care about and that are supported by the decision-makers I need to reach.
11. After I obtain my board seat, I will actively help qualified women and minorities to take their seats around the corporate board table.

(To learn more about OnBoard Bootcamp, please visit www.onboardbootcamp.com)

My First Board — JAN BABIAK

"My first board experience was on the other side of the table, because I spent a lot of time in boardrooms as an advisor with Ernst & Young. But I've always been a long-term planner — I had my first life plan when I was eight years old! — and I had started thinking about and planning for board work for more than a decade before I was offered my first seat. When the time came, I started talking with search firms and with people who had 'gone plural' (that is, serving on multiple boards). What should I do over the course of my career to make me a more attractive board candidate when the time was right? Years later, one of those search firms approached me about a board opportunity that became my first independent director role.

My very first board meeting was a little different from most. After a 30-year career, I had promised my husband we would spend two months traveling around South America and Antarctica. The board role was offered after the cruise was booked so I suggested joining the board effective after the trip. They wanted me to start immediately. We were smack dab in the middle of this cruise for my first meeting — but I kept my promise to my husband by agreeing with my new board to attend the board and committee meetings via a two-day phone call from Rio de Janeiro (while my husband gamely agreed to entertain himself on Ipanema Beach).

CAN YOU BE GOOGLED?

"For most of history, Anonymous was a woman."

– Virginia Wolfe

How can you go about making yourself board ready? The first step is "don't be shy" — put your information out in the open. Getting on a board is like running a political campaign: you have to make your name known. Can you be googled? If you can't, that's a problem. To gain visibility, consider writing and publishing papers, speaking at conferences, and networking with people who can promote your interests. Volunteer for bigger assignments and become active in your industry.

Women have a tendency to work hard and hope to get noticed: that's not the right approach. So, self-promotion is a key quality for the board-ambitious. Take every opportunity throughout your career — at business receptions, luncheons, or dinners — to tell other executives, "Keep me in mind should one of your boards need a woman with my expertise." Be very succinct about what your "value add" would be to the board. Have you helped other companies through strategic mergers? Have you helped companies grow? Have you helped them downsize? Let people know.

Also, you need to be able to sell yourself to a recruiter or board member in an "elevator pitch" in which you quickly (in less than two minutes) highlight your strengths. Show one credential that makes you stand out. What do you want to be remembered for?

"If you're on a not-for-profit board, tell the other directors you're seeking a public seat — that's a great networking opportunity."

Judi North | a director of Acuity Brands, Community Health Systems, and Lumos Networks, co-chair of WCD Atlanta Chapter and an advisory board member of WCD

ACTION TIPS

Come up with a list of the 10 companies whose board you'd like to join.

Get to know the board members, first by getting their names from the company website. Google each one and review their CV's for a potential linkage: are they on a not-for-profit board you're interested in? Are they alumni of the same school as you or your children? Use your connections at your networking groups to see if they can introduce you to a board member. Remember, the large majority of placements are based on existing relationships with the board and/or CEO.

Let everyone know you're looking for board positions at particular companies and/or certain industries.

Become a board member at a not-for-profit organization, but only if you believe in its cause. This will help you get valuable experience, especially if the board is structured like a corporate one with committees, for example. Once on the board, work hard, be engaged, and join a committee. Your fellow board members are likely to be on boards of companies that interest you – let them see how good you are and you will be on another board.

Be patient as you start the formal search; on average, it takes more than two years to be selected as a board director, and the first one is the hardest. Also, be realistic. A Fortune 100 company isn't likely to be your first board, unless you are the CEO of another Fortune 100 company. Small, for-profit companies and advisory boards are great starting places.

My First Board — DENISE FLETCHER

"My success as a director is built on a strong corporate career with touches of coincidences, like being at the right place, at the right time, and networking. Twenty years ago, I bumped into a woman — literally! — In Grand Central Station, New York. As we tried to help each other, we started chatting. Eventually, we became friends. Her husband was a senior executive at an investment company and a member of the board of directors of one of the companies it had invested in. He contacted me because the board was looking for a director with finance expertise. By then, I was well known, as I had become the corporate treasurer of The New York Times Company in 1980 — that company's first female and youngest ever corporate officer.

"So, Software Etc. Stores was my first board. Eventually, after I became CFO of MasterCard, a role that gave me additional visibility because of the company's global brand and huge technology base, I was invited to join my first Fortune 500 company board, Unisys, a worldwide information technology company. The contact was made through Catalyst, a not-for-profit organization dedicated to the advancement of women in the corporate world.

"Over time, I served on many boards and became a member of WomenCorporateDirectors, an organization whose network has helped me achieve my goals."

WE TALK TO A DIVERSITY CHAMPION: PAUL POLMAN

WomenCorporateDirectors honored Paul Polman, CEO of Unilever, with its WCD Visionary Award for Leadership. The award recognizes a top-performing company whose board includes three or more women for serving as a role model in both corporate leadership and best governance practices. Unilever has five women among its 12 non-executive board members.

› Why are women important to Unilever?

"When you look around the world and at the issues that society faces, you find that if you invest in women, you get the highest returns. Where people are moving into the middle classes, usually it is because of women starting to work. Take Africa, for example. When women work, 90 percent of their earnings are reinvested in their families or in their communities. That's why we have to invest in women if we want to address the big social issues. It makes sense for the world and it makes sense for our business model — with 85 percent of our growth at Unilever coming from emerging markets, and 70-80 percent of purchase decisions and use of our products by women. This is enlightened self-interest."

› How are you bringing women along in your pipeline?

"You have to have robust programs in place. You set your targets — from recruiting to mentoring, tracking, and accountability. I set a personal example. One of my own personal targets is linked to our gender balance objectives, which reflect the tone I set from the top. We also hire from the outside and insist on a significant over-representation of women. This has brought Unilever an enormous amount of knowledge and gained us a lot of respect. Right now we are about 45 percent women in manager levels, 30 percent in higher levels, and almost 50 percent at the board level. This is quite a dramatic change from where we were a few years ago."

› What big trends do you see?

"First, a change in the power balance in the world. The leadership role that the U.S. has played, and should be proud of, in the global economy is shrinking back; China and India are not willing to take on that role. So, for the next decade we'll see a power vacuum at the political level.

Second, the end of the era of abundance. We are facing planetary boundaries that are enormous, and these constraints are even before two billion more people come into this world. This is why we have come up with our Unilever Sustainable Business model.

Third, what I call the 'consumer in charge.' Consumers increasingly are discovering their power. You saw that with the Arab Spring and the Occupy Wall Street movements. You see it in the digitization of society. With one billion people now on Facebook, that means that after China and India Facebook is the 'third country.' In the absence of politicians taking charge, consumers are crying out and demanding change.

"These three trends are converging at a rapid rate. "

A FIRST IMPRESSION MATTERS (SO DOES A SECOND AND THIRD)

"Always be a first-rate version of yourself, instead of a second-rate version of somebody else. "

– Judy Garland

How do you present your skills and expertise, your experiences and perspective, your confidence and ambitions? Seeking a board position is not the same as looking for a job. Interviewing for a job is all about showing your leadership skills. Interviewing for a director's position is all about showing how well you'd fit into the board's culture. That's why you need to take these extra steps:

Fill in gaps in your experience (but do not invent credentials). For example, if you lack depth in financial literacy, you could take a university course: many business schools, including Stanford and Wharton, offer programs where actual and potential directors learn the basics of finance, governance, and ethics. Then, write your resume as a "board bio" (follow the OnBoard Bootcamp framework on page 87).

Stay current. In his *Directors & Boards* article, "Be the Person That Boards Are Looking For," Ralph Walkling recommends investing "a small portion of your savings in companies that interest you and follow their performance. After all, one mechanism for aligning the interests of owners and managers is to have executives become owners themselves. Study 10-Ks — they are the board's primary vehicle for communicating results to the world. Learn some basics of corporate finance, investments, and financial markets, and develop a financial vocabulary."

Put the spotlight on yourself. Videotape your next presentation, or even a staff meeting, and then watch yourself specifically to see what non-verbal clues you send to others. Are you constantly looking at your notes when someone else is speaking? If so, you may as well holdup a sign saying, "Bored. Waiting for my turn." Ask a colleague for the hard answers to some tough questions: "Do I give off any negative vibes? Do I have any signature phrases or gestures? What bad habits do I display in meetings or during presentations?"

When you get an interview, ask the right questions. For example, "What skill sets are you looking for on this board? What is it about my background that interests you?" (Read more in the section, "Life is an interview" on page 103). But also provide the right content. The perfect end to the conversation would be the questioner saying, "Wow, I would have paid for that information."

A BOARD BIO IS WRITTEN IN LEADERSHIP LANGUAGE

"Our work is the presentation of our capabilities."

– Edward Gibbon

A board biography is not the same as a resume or CV. Rather, it frames your accomplishments and capabilities in leadership language. In your board biography, you want to sell yourself for success.

Here are some examples of leadership language:

Worked on a project	» Team leader for high priority project
Ran XYZ business	» Profit and loss responsibility for $50M business
Studied the impact of	» Completed rigorous analysis of issues and implications for the CEO
On technical team	» Key player in task force to develop marketing program for high-tech products
MBA, Columbia	» MBA, Columbia with major in finance and accounting

Here is the board biography template from OnBoard Bootcamp:

Biography for [INSERT NAME]

[INSERT NAME] has more than 30 years of executive management experience in a wide variety of challenging environments: start-up, rapid growth, turnaround, consolidating, Internet, regulated, and traditional businesses. Her background includes serving as a CEO, president and COO, public and private company board member; she's been a proven, top operating executive in businesses ranging from $100 million to billions in revenue.

[INSERT NAME] has earned the reputation of being a talented leader in companies undergoing dramatic change by creating a positive work atmosphere in which open communications, a sense of urgency, and rapid execution of well-understood plans lead to bottom-line, measurable success. [INSERT NAME] especially loves building teams. She has always been active in the community and has served on numerous philanthropic boards.

Today, [INSERT NAME] is focused on a portfolio of corporate/community boards and advisory activities.

Current Corporate Boards and Advisory Boards

[INSERT COMPANY], a mature, private company which is the leading, global provider of customer insight management tools and online technology solutions for top consumer brands (board member, 2010 to present)

[INSERT COMPANY], a family-owned business which is a top online XXX site. [INSERT NAME] advises the father-son team in organizational and management development, business process and scaling, strategy, and mentoring (executive advisor, 2004 to present)

CURRENT NON-PROFIT BOARDS

[INSERT ORGANIZATION], a top ranked, private, coed, school (grades 6-12) with a strong emphasis on academics and human development (2004-2009, co-chair of the 75th Anniversary Capital Campaign; 2006-08, President of the Board; 2008-10, Chair of the Board; Trustee, 2004 to present)

[INSERT ORGANIZATION], a leading regional/teaching hospital in XXX (board member, 1998 to present)

FORMER CORPORATE BOARDS

[INSERT COMPANY], ownership type, revenues, description of business, role (advisor, Trustee, NXD) and dates of service.

MAJOR OPERATING EXPERIENCE

[Include narrative summary of career in reverse chronological order (three to four paragraphs). Provide a brief overview of companies, roles, responsibilities, accomplishments, and reporting structure. Remember to include reasons and motivations for transitions]

Until early 2004, [INSERT NAME] was the COO for XXX. The company is widely recognized as a star Internet performer. This publicly-traded company redefined how to succeed in online advertising by creating "paid search" and built a highly scalable, profitable, and fast growing global business. During [INSERT NAME]'s three-year tenure as COO, the company experienced hyper growth, including a jump of annual revenues from $100 million to $1.2 billion, a shift from negative profits to 10 consecutive, profitable quarters, an increase in annual paid leads from 750 million to three (3) billion, an increase in advertisers from 37,000 to 110,000, and an expansion into international markets (from one to twelve). In the fall of 2003, XXX was sold to XXX for $1.6 billion.

From [date] to [date], [INSERT NAME] was the president and COO of XXX. She joined this start-up in a classic "adult supervision" role when the company received $32 million in venture funding. XXX became the largest XXX service on the Internet and was eventually sold to XXX, creating the clearly dominant player in the space.

Before [date], [INSERT NAME] had spent most of her career in financial services. She thrived at XXX where she spent eleven years. Her final position was as a management committee member and executive vice president (EVP) responsible for retail at the $58 billion bank. She managed $1 billion in revenue, 4,000 employees, 403 stores, and a 1,000-person sales force. Other positions at XXX included EVP and area manager for XXX, SVP and chief marketing officer, and executive assistant to the chairman and CEO.

Following the hostile takeover of XXX in 1996, the consolidation in banking accelerated. [INSERT NAME] was recruited in succession to the two largest S&L's in the country, XXX and XXX, as the EVP and management committee member responsible for retail and business banking. In both cases, she helped transform these traditional thrifts into commercial banks and positioned the companies for sale. At each company, she managed retail and business banking and had responsibility for $1 billion in revenue, 5,000 employees, over 500 stores across multiple states, call centers, loan processing centers, as well as marketing, product management, and delivery departments. XXX was sold after overcoming a hostile takeover attempt in 1997. XXX was sold in 1998. Prior to her career in financial services, [INSERT NAME] was a product manager with XXX and a management consultant with XXX.

EDUCATION/OTHER

[INSERT NAME] graduated from XXX. She earned a BA in _____ (include honors) from XXX and an MBA from XXX.

On the personal front, [INSERT NAME] was raised in Maryland. and had several internships with the federal government. She has resided in [INSERT CITY and STATE] for nearly 30 years with her husband, XXX, a [INSERT CAREER]. They have three adult children.

CONTACT INFORMATION:
[INSERT NAME]
HOME ADDRESS
EMAIL
PHONE:

Board Bio

ACTION TIPS

Review your current CV to find any experience gaps; once they're identified, strategize how you can get the experience you're missing (including at your current company).

Understand the skills most valued by boards. Currently trending are experience as a CEO (obviously), CFO, or CPA; experience in BRIC and ASEAN countries; expertise in CAMS (Cloud, Analytics, Mobility and/or Social Media); and other technology experience, such as data security.

If you speak more than one language, highlight that skill near the top of your biography.

Be sure to give yourself some time to get the experience and expertise you're missing.

Change your elevator speech and resume to showcase the experiences that a board member would need or admire. For example, if you're a great project manager, you're probably great at strategy. Say so! Think through initiatives you've led and get them into your go-to discussion points.

SUCCESSFUL PEOPLE SWEAT THE SMALL STUFF

"The details are not the details. They make the design."
– Charles Eames

In a world in which we are urged to see the big picture and capture the brass ring, where the speed of change accelerates with every new website and technological tool, it too often feels as if we don't have the time for details. The small cues, the simple gestures, and the random acts of kindness that give life texture and meaning — they're too often overlooked or ignored.

But in reality no one gets ahead without "sweating the small stuff"; it really *does* matter.

Check that email again before sending it — that says a lot about how careful and meticulous you would be on a larger project. Learn to proofread the details in your personal and professional life: read your speech, report, and business correspondence out loud. It's the only surefire way to catch an error.

Taking the time to give a compliment or being attuned to a colleague's or customer's body language are not inconsequential actions — they are clear signs that a person recognizes that small facts and actions can be powerful agents of change and growth. Indra Nooyi, CEO of PepsiCo, wrote personal letters to the parents of her C-level reports, praising their long hours and hard work; as a result, the executives were willing to give even more to the effort.

My First Board — CATHY ALLEN

"For a number of years, I was the CEO for a financial services consortium called BITS, which looked at how emerging technologies would impact the industry. My first board, Stewart Title, was looking for someone who had a financial services background and understood emerging technologies. My second board was an electric utility — this was a good fit for me because I had done work on critical infrastructure after 9/11, so I understood the industry. Also, I understood public policy within a regulated industry. My last board, which is a regional financial services board, pulled all of that together.

"I'm a big believer in getting to know people one-on-one. Even before I attended my first board meeting, I interviewed, or talked to, or called every single board member, as well as the company's general counsel and senior executives. I did my due diligence in understanding not only how the company operated but also the politics of the board.

"So from the start, I had a good sense of the people, of the 'hot button' issues, and of the board's working style. In my first board meeting, I listened and watched the body language and interactions among the members. By the second meeting, I was ready to participate because I knew what was going on at an intellectual level, an emotional level, and an interest level."

SOMETIMES WHAT ISN'T SAID, SAYS IT ALL

"The most important thing in communication is hearing what isn't said."

— Peter Drucker

People "speak" in all kinds of ways. That's why it's important to become fluent in body language, especially now, when face-to-face time seems to be shrinking as we rely more heavily on electronic communication in the workplace and in our day-to-day lives. That means we have to glean as much as we possibly can from our personal encounters, because the unspoken cues people give in person can never be replicated in emails, text messages, or even phone calls.

One of our favorite war stories from Madison Avenue is how Charlotte Beers, a pioneering woman in advertising, won the Sears account. Back in the 1970s, Sears was all about power tools. As a woman pitching to Sears, Charlotte felt at a distinct disadvantage. So, five minutes into the crucial meeting with the Sears honchos, Charlotte silently pulled out an electric drill, took it apart, and put it back together without even dropping a screw. Needless to say, she won the business.

As an experiment, try a little sensory deprivation by wearing earplugs on the bus or subway. What do you notice about the other passengers? What are they saying without words? When you're in a meeting, notice the little cues, such as how people place themselves around a conference table or whether someone is smiling just with her mouth or her whole face.

Paying attention to signals requires good emotional and social "muscles;" with focus and repetition these can be developed (just like biceps and triceps). One important inquiry: Who is introverted and who is extroverted? By discovering this one distinction, you'll be better able to understand each person's communication style and know how to interact with him or her.

You might feel a little awkward as you begin to pay more attention to the behavior and conversations of people around you. But with practice, you will get better at reading between the lines and even at noticing chances to make yourself known by doing more than expected. People will remember you if you do, and you will feel better and more engaged with those around you as well.

SMALL BEGINNINGS LEAD TO BIG ENDINGS

"From a small seed a mighty trunk may grow."

— Aeschylus

When it comes to mapping your journey to a corporate board, it's a good idea to start small. For example, consider serving on the board of a non-profit organization (these boards often include corporate directors). This work increases your visibility, showcases your capacity for working in a group, widens your network, and expands future opportunities. Join a committee to gain skills and confidence. Early successes and the gratification that they bring, will spur you to the next task and the next.

Sherry Barrat advises women to hang out with directors and CEOs, because they need to see you in action, doing board-room type activities: "Let's say you're a division manager in your company. Perhaps you've put together and directed an advisory board. Or maybe you've worked as a director of, or on a committee for, a non-profit. In such settings, people can see how you think and how you lead: How do you run a meeting? How do you build consensus? How do you handle conflict? How do you move the ball? Would you have good chemistry with the other directors on a corporate board? If directors know you, they'll think of you when an opportunity comes to their attention."

ADVISORY BOARDS: A GOOD WAY TO SHOW YOUR STUFF

In today's complex world, companies are turning to "experts for hire" in the form of advisory boards comprised of people with extensive skills, relevant experience, and a pragmatic perspective. An advisory board brings together valuable talent and new thinking without risk or liability for the enterprise (read more about advisory boards on page 162).

Everyone's a winner: The company gets expert guidance and insights, while the advisory board members get an opportunity to know the company's leadership and to demonstrate their strengths as potential future directors. Of course, some advisory board members do not want to become directors, but still enjoy contributing their skills in guiding a company's decision-making.

BEING NICE IS A VIRTUE (YES, THAT'S RIGHT, *NICE*)

"Constant kindness can accomplish much. As the sun makes ice melt, kindness causes misunderstanding, mistrust, and hostility to evaporate."

— Albert Schweitzer

Some executives think that "being nice" means being a pushover, a doormat, a wimp. Not true! "Being nice" really means being consistently generous and amicable, open to the ideas of others, patient in words and deeds, and willing to give others the benefit of the doubt.

Sullivan & Cromwell, a staid law firm in New York, learned the value of niceness the hard way. For two years running, the firm had a turnover rate of more than 30 percent. Compensation was not the issue, nor was promotion rates or health benefits. But the young attorneys did not feel appreciated. When *American Lawyer* published its annual review of mid-level associates, Sullivan & Cromwell ranked near the bottom of 163 firms surveyed.

So, the firm's partners decided to introduce two phrases that had been sorely missing from the firm's lexicon: "Please" and "Thank you." Senior partners began making small talk with junior associates in the halls and elevators, praising them for jobs well done or politely asking (rather than demanding) whether they would stay late for an urgent meeting. It didn't cost a dime, but the effort to be gracious, respectful, and polite to everyone in the firm, regardless of their positions in the hierarchy, had a powerful effect. When the next *American Lawyer* review came around, Sullivan & Cromwell was rated the top law employer among New York firms — all because of the power of being nice.

If nothing else, being nice is central to networking. Look through your appointment calendar and make a list of five people you're scheduled to meet with in the coming weeks. Then, find out one casual bit of information about each person say, where her daughter goes to college or whether she likes to play golf and drop it into your next conversation. (If you've met the person before, drop a fact or two in your Outlook address file, so that you can recall it for next time.) By paying attention to "niceties" in face-to-face interactions, you'll make a great impression and maybe even a great friend.

SO IS BEING CURIOUS

"We keep moving forward, opening new doors, and doing new things, because we're curious and curiosity keeps leading us down new paths."

— Walt Disney

As part of your readiness campaign, nurture the quality of curiosity about others. When in conversation, be genuinely interested. When you listen and ask questions, you show the other person that you respect his or her point of view. Small talk is anything but idle chatter. In fact, it's the glue that cements many relationships, and relationships cement the active networking necessary to making your ambitions known. The more curious you are during a conversation, the more positive the outcome.

Potential directors should also be lifetime learners, eager to expand their knowledge, gain insights, and fill in any gaps in their skill sets. When you do get the chance to serve on a board (non-profit or corporate), you need to be fully prepared to make meaningful, effective contributions. Being a curious, natural learner, you'll have to be comfortable asking questions, no matter how seemingly dumb or trivial it's the best direct way to solve problems while they're still small and manageable.

"A woman wanting to be on a board should build skills beyond her core expertise. Everyone on a board of directors was invited because he or she is knowledgeable; each has accomplished things, and all are (or should be) open to expanding their expertise so they can be comfortable contributing on issues that are outside their comfort zone. Building a board that's interested in new ways of looking at the world is absolutely essential for being competitive in the 21st century."

Deborah Wince-Smith | President of the Global Federation of Competitiveness Councils, a director of NanoMech, and Vice Chair of Thought Leadership and an advisory board member of WCD

A SMART IDEA: INCREASE YOUR CQ

"Globalism began as a vision of a world with free trade, shared prosperity, and open borders. These are good, even noble things to aim for."

– Deepak Chopra

What's CQ? Cultural Quotient. In a global world, your ability to "get" other people's traditions and expectations is really important.

In their *Harvard Business Review* article, Christopher Earley, Dean and James Brooke Henderson Professor of Management at Purdue University's Krannert School of Management and Elaine Mosakowski, Professor of Management at Purdue University's Krannert School of Management, coined the term as "the ability to cope with national, corporate and vocational cultures. CQ is the ability to make sense of unfamiliar contexts and then blend in." Thinkquest.org refines that definition: CQ is "one's ability to recognize cultural differences through knowledge and mindfulness, and behave appropriately when facing people from other cultures."

As our world shrinks, and as more businesses are forced to think globally (whether because of customers, suppliers, or competitors), CQ matters. A potential board director should understand the social customs and business practices of other regions, countries, and ethnicities.

Carolyn Chan, an independent consultant and former founding co-chair of the WCD Singapore Chapter, shares her view of why CQ is so important: "The world is flat to borrow from *New York Times* columnist, Thomas Friedman and now, more and more people have to work across borders. In the '70s, the idea of leadership was a little simpler: people could see whom they managed, literally; they sat in the same office; they were in the same communities; they went to the same church; and their kids went to the same school. Now, we are managing and leading people we've never seen before; they're half way around the world, and we have no idea of their background, their values and belief systems.

"Cultural intelligence is the ability to understand the impact of an action on another person's behavior, even when there's some kind of distance between the two. Improving your CQ begins with increasing awareness of your own culture's worldview, your own attitude towards differences, your own assumption and biases. Then, you're ready to gain knowledge of other practices and worldviews, thereby developing the competence to understand, communicate, and be effective in new areas.

"Say a company wants to do business in China or India. What does the board know about these countries and their cultures? Maybe the next director should be Chinese or Indian. What if it wants to expand into a market that's dominated by women consumers? Are there woman on the board? I like to tell boards 'get equipped, get focused, get clear' and imagine how others could contribute."

10 tips for a higher CQ (developed with the help of Phyllis Campbell, Chairman of the Pacific Northwest of JPMorgan, lead director of Alaska Air Group, a director of Nordstrom and Vice Chair of Asia for WCD.)

Stay focused on the big picture. Doing business globally means more than developing strategies with business partners in other first-world countries. It also means cultivating relationships in emerging markets, which may not share a US "bottom line" perspective. As advisors, directors need to expand their own (and their company's) perspectives and spheres of influence.

Appreciate the world's deep well of human capital. If the world were a village with just 99 people, 60 would be Asian, 14 African, 12 European, and eight Latin American. Only five would come from the United States and Canada. Only 18 would be white. Thirty-two would be Christian and 67 non-Christian. Diversity enables a bigger world view in decision-making.

Look for common ground. Developing economies are unpredictable. For example, governments throughout Africa and the Middle East require different levels of regulation. Directors need to be able to analyze each potential partner's capabilities to determine a likely return on investment. Some industries may be particularly rocky overseas, and efforts should focus on optimal results.

Acknowledge perceptions about the United States. Directors for US-based companies need to be aware that Americans are often perceived as uninformed, outspoken workaholics. Of course, perception is not necessarily reality. Represent your company's true values when doing business internationally.

Go where the growth is. The center of gravity in the global economy is shifting toward Asia, Africa, and the Middle East. According to the article "Top Growers" in *The Economist*, it was predicted that the top five fastest-growing economies in the world in 2014 would be South Sudan, Mongolia, Macao, Sierra Leone and Turkmenistan. In the Middle East and Africa, states and countries are spending billions on developing infrastructure while working to expand possibilities for foreign investment.

Expect the unexpected. As they develop, countries constantly reform their policies, and that means US companies need to be very adaptable. Researching a country's regulations beforehand saves time and reduces risk in choosing where to establish relationships.

Understand local customs and business practices. This shows that a director cares about a company, not just strategically, but also as an organization of people with different backgrounds and beliefs. Small ways to make a good impression include, researching local holidays, observing protocols for greetings, and printing business cards in the local language. When you're introduced, should you shake hands, bow, or kiss? The right answer makes all the difference.

Be patient. Expect transactions and decision-making to take longer (sometimes much longer) with many delays along the way. In the Middle East, it's common for business leaders to engage in long discussions and lengthy meetings before making a decision. Government regulations can always slow things down.

Form your own opinion. If people did business only in countries that get good reviews in the daily news coverage, no one would do any business at all. What may be true for select groups is not true for all. Don't play up to the stereotype of "ignorant Americans" by assuming anything.

Recognize that relationships matter. In the Middle East, the first part of a meeting is getting to know each other, which can include talking about politics and global events. It's considered rude to jump right to business. Also, since face-to-face interaction is valued, don't send an e-mail to follow up a meeting: pick up the phone.

"Companies doing business in Asia or who employ many Asians might benefit importantly from Asian directors who can help read and navigate cultural and other unspoken signals that could influence major business decisions and hiring. For example, so often with Asian companies what is intended is not the obvious message, but a reflection of past interactions or an expectation in the future. A courtesy or sign of respect can reflect that a positive relationship is taking hold; the parties can begin to trust and depend on each other. But if projected slightly differently, a gesture might signal that there is no chance of a future relationship, so it's best to limit one's exposure. When building a relationship in Asia, a willingness to make concessions in the short term can be hugely rewarding in the long term."

Lulu Wang | a director of MetLife Insurance Company and Asia Society, Overseer of Columbia Business School, an advisory council member of U.S. Trust, and an advisory board member of WCD

LIFE IS AN INTERVIEW

"The meeting of two personalities is like the contact of two chemical substances: If there is any reaction, both are transformed."

— Carl Jung

Your board bio gets you in the door, but it's the interview that gets you to the table. Interviewing for a spot as a director is different from interviewing for a job. It's not just about performance; it's about your compatibility with the other board members. Candidates need to go beyond functional requirements to show they can play on the team. After all, the whole is greater than the sum of its parts. (Of course, being a team player doesn't necessarily mean being agreeable all the time; some of the highest performing companies have extremely contentious boards that regard dissent as an obligation and that treat no subject as off limits.)

Here are tips for interviewing for a board so you can put your best self forward:

Before an interview

Take some time to become familiar with the audience. Before you have any asks about your upcoming interviews, do your homework on all of the company executives and board members — you can get most of the info on their webpage and Google. Know their names, background, current position and/or committees they are on for this company and other boards. Meeting organizers and search firms expect you to have this done.

Melissa Means, Managing Director at Pearl Meyer & Partners, suggests spending some time meeting with the head of human resources during the recruitment process (in addition to the CEO and other members of the board) to learn more about the company and, more importantly, its people. "Don't overlook the value that interacting with a head of human resources may provide," she says. If you can, talk to the meeting organizer or search firm to find out as much as possible about the interview participants:

- Who are they?
- How many will be attending?
- Will they attend the entire session or part?

- What information do they want? What do they need?
- Is there a perception about what your value and background can bring to the board?
- What is their work background and education level?
- Should you be aware of points of view or local customs?

Think about what a board member is evaluated on. As a board member, you'll be expected to be accountable (that is, make the commitment of time to visit stores and plants, meet with employees, suppliers and officers of the company, often before or after business hours), attend meetings faithfully and be well-prepared, actively serve on committees, be available for special projects and informal interactions with board members and senior management, and participate in discussions.

These expectations suggest that you should demonstrate your ability to take initiative (in promoting ideas and making inquiries), to make thoughtful contributions to corporate governance issues, to ask tough questions that move deliberations and decision-making forward, to be a sharpshooter (not a hip shooter), to disagree without being disagreeable, and to share information. Remember Noah's rule: There are no prizes for predicting rain, only for building arks.

During the interview

- Take command of the room by being confident in your self
- Arouse interest in you and your qualifications
- Focus your enthusiasm on important issues
- Explain why the company is important to you
- Say what you mean and mean what you say
- Sell your ideas (including the idea of you) by arguing your points with strong and appropriate examples
- Get action by explicitly stating how you/your expertise can benefit the company
- Encourage your audience to act

More hints to boost your interviewing style
- Allow enough time to prepare your material
- Prepare several key message points that you want to emphasize in the interview
- Use a strong "grabber" to establish a purpose, provide continuity, and reinforce points
- Anticipate major questions and prepare answers to them
- When a person asks a question, maintain eye contact. Reply simply and directly. End every answer on a positive/upbeat note. If you don't have an answer, either refer the question to an expert (if one is present) or say you'll look into the matter and get back with an answer (then, be sure you do)
- Make all body movement and gestures work for you. Be aware of your posture
- Even after the formal interview process has ended, you are still "on stage"
- Most importantly, expect to do well

Interviewing DON'Ts
- Talk about politics or religion
- Wait too long to answer a question or respond with an answer that's too long
- Make comments that call into question your judgment or integrity
- Gaze off, yawn, or look bored
- Ask a question about something anyone would know by reading the annual report
- Get emotional or angry
- Give the impression of being a loner or prima donna
- Be too pushy, too smart, too aggressive, or too passive
- Be too talkative or too quiet

Dressing for the interview
- Always look neat and professional
- Never wear something new (you don't know whether or how it might pull, and looking self-conscious will detract from your credibility)
- Look like the best version of yourself rather than copying someone else's style
- Dress for business, not for a dinner party

After the interview

- Talk to your source or search executive to get feedback
- Write a thoughtful "thank you" letter to nominating committee members and other interviewers
- If any lingering questions can be addressed effectively in a letter, send one. If there are questions that require documentation, ask how much time you have and pull together a memo. If there's more information you can send on an issue discussed, include it.

Even if you don't win a specific director spot, the interviewer/search executive will have other opportunities. So making a good impression still counts.

My First Board — SHERRY BARRAT

"When I was in my mid-40s, I was the CEO of a region of Northern Trust (but this was still a middle manager job). I had been courting, as a prospective client, the man who was at the time CEO of a large company headquartered nearby; over two or three years, I had met with him a lot. One day, he called me up and said 'Sherry, I'd like to take you to lunch.' I thought, 'Wow, this is it — he's finally giving us his business.' After lunch, over coffee, he said, 'Alright, let's get down to business.'

Then he said, 'We would like you to come on our board.' I was so stunned I doubted I'd really heard what he said. I remember replying, 'If I say yes, will you say yes?'

"Looking back, I realize I had readied myself for the offer: I had served on a few boards of non-profits with the CEO and with one of his other Directors. So, he did know me in that context. Also, Northern Trust has always had a very good reputation: being a leader in the company meant I was also a leader in the community (and the CEO wanted someone local). Finally, the board's one woman was leaving, and the CEO wanted to replace her with another woman. I give him a lot of credit, because back then corporate boards tended to be 'old boys' clubs. He was determined to make the board contemporary."

IS THIS THE RIGHT BOARD FOR ME?

"A good puzzle, it's a fair thing. Nobody is lying. It's very clear, and the problem depends just on you."

– Erno Rubik

To find out whether you and a board are a good match, you need to know about the company: what it does, how it operates, and what it stands for. Finding the right board is a little like solving Rubik's cube: all the pieces have to line up.

In her *NACD Directorship* article, "Questions to Ask Before Joining a Board," Ellen B. Richstone, a director of eMagin Corporation, Bioamber Inc., Paxeramed Corp, and Pro Teck Valuation Services, says that "the hardest questions are the least measurable, but equally and sometimes more important than the measurable ones." Ask these questions when evaluating a board service opportunity:

- What are the company's strategic, long-term plans? Does it have a robust strategic planning process that includes rigorous risk assessments? Take a close look at the company's competitive position, opportunities for expansion, and the regulatory environment. To understand the company's financial strength, take a close look at cash flow, debt levels, and operating requirements. Does the company collect competitive intelligence? If so, how does it use this information?
- What are the company's products/services and historical performance? Look for answers in annual reports and financial statements, paying particular attention to management's discussion and analyses. Also, use internet search engines and personal networks to find out about any problems, including litigation. Richstone suggests researching market size, growth rate, and any increase or decline in market share, while looking at key market demand drivers and expected new product development over the next three to five years. Are new geographical areas or sales channels being considered?
- Is the company sensitive to customers? A focus on customer satisfaction should be enterprise-wide.
- How does the company identify and discuss risk? Are internal controls in place to protect the company's reputation and prevent fraud, not just in its US

businesses, but also in its global operations? Before agreeing to join a board, you should check out any regulations affecting the company's operations, country by country. Of course, you'll want to know about any pending or threatened litigation or investigations (read the "ABCs of fraud and misconduct" on page 178).

- What's the tone at the top? How well does everyone work together? Do decision makers listen well and consider conflicting points of view? Richstone recalls one company that matched board members with an executive, expecting the two to meet and speak regularly. The matches were rotated so that over time the director would know the entire executive team, thereby improving communication and collaboration.
- How does the company attract, motivate, and retain talent? Is employee turnover high? If so, why? Employee survey results reveal attitudes toward ethics, strategy, and growth.
- Perhaps the most important question of all: Where would you fit on the board? What gaps is the board trying to fill? Which committee would make the best use of your background and skills?

Of course, no company is perfect. But before joining a board, you should know exactly what kind of "not perfect" you can tolerate. Don't hesitate to trust your intuition: What kind of "vibe" do you get about the company, its management team, and the other directors? After finishing your due diligence, you should feel confident in the company's culture and values.

My First Board — HENRIETTA FORE

"Twenty years ago I was running a privately held steel company in California. I became interested in serving on a public corporate board. There are many practices a private company can learn from a public company and vice-versa. I began talking to a number of friends and search firms. Then I found Catalyst, a women's organization that had a superb recruiter, Donna Manning, who was leading the placement of women on corporate boards. When an opening occurred that fit the company's needs and my experience, I did my first interview. I found I loved the company and the issues. That became my first public board.

"My father had owned many companies and through him and many years of operations and analysis of acquisitions, I knew about governance procedures, how to look at a company's financials, stock, products, services and leadership. From these companies and from nonprofit work, I knew about the different roles of directors and of management. Board candidates tend to know the management side first; then when we become directors, our roles shift. With my experience, I could see the company through the eyes of a director and also through the eyes of management. This interesting interplay of board and management can be very positive for corporate performance excellence, and is a responsibility of every corporate director.

"I attended the Board of Directors' course at Stanford University to learn more about public companies' processes, federal regulations and oversight, compensation and audit. These are essentials for incoming board members. If you are interested in board service, think deeply about the companies, industries, sizes and geographies that both interest you and to which you can bring added value. Then tell all your friends."

ACTION TIPS

In deciding whether a board is a good fit, begin by doing your homework:

Know the company's financials, products and services
Look at the annual report, financial statements, markets for the company's securities, past or pending litigation, internal controls, and management's discussions and analyses.

Investigate the intangibles
What is the company's culture? Look at employee surveys to find out attitudes toward ethics, strategy, and growth. Explore reasons behind high or low attrition, such as a competitive or soft job market. Is the company a great place to work or an unpleasant environment?

Research the company's strategic plans
What is the state of the company's markets (growing or shrinking)? Are there recognized or untapped opportunities for future expansion? How strict is the regulatory environment? What are the potential global risks?

Assess the C-suite's and board directors' capabilities
If possible, meet with CEO, COO, CFO, general counsel and board members. Do they have the right qualities and intellectual capital? Do they listen and consider conflicting points of view? How well do the board members work together?

Where would you fit on the board?
What gaps is the board trying to fill? Which committee(s) would make the best use of your background and skills?

EXTEND YOUR REACH, AND CAST YOUR NET WIDE

"When you build relationships of trust, you can then bring your ideas to those relationships and you'll get more done. You'll have more influence."
– Denise Morrison, President, CEO and a director at Campbell Soup Company, a director at MetLife, Inc., and Catalyst

In today's world, global networks — financial, social, and business — are more important than ever. We have reached a point where we are competing with everyone, everywhere for everything. Individuals need networks and connections and relationships to get ahead. Networking and connectivity cannot lag. Instead of turning inward, we need to enlarge our circle of advisors, our perspective, and our spheres of influence to better understand the new world, and to become better executives and future board members.

Networking gives a person visibility; it's a good way to "get on the radar" for a board position.

While the networking styles of men and women differ, everyone wanting to get to the boardroom needs to build deep relationships and invest in social capital, which means building a posse (trusted people you can turn to when the going gets rough), having access to a "big ideas" crowd (people who can keep you mentally fresh), and participating in a regenerative community (family and friends with whom you can share a laugh, a meal, and a story).

Networking allows others to vouch that you are helpful, that you are constructive, and that you contribute well. That's why it's important that your network both supports and challenges you. These relationships should help you gain influence, broaden your expertise, learn new skills, and find purpose and balance. The result of networking should be more learning, less bias in decision making, and greater personal growth and balance.

"Pause and look around: who might be helpful in your journey? Get out there and meet people. Be active in the right organizations. Engage in the community: CEOs are often working for charities, schools, or arts groups. Serving on a not-for-profit board can be a good first step toward a corporate board position."

Pat McKay | a Partner and Managing Director of Templeton & Company LLP, a trustee of Committee for Economic Development, an advisory board member and CFO of WCD and co-chair of WCD South Florida Chapter

A MENTOR WILL TALK *WITH* YOU; A SPONSOR WILL TALK *ABOUT* YOU. YOU NEED BOTH

"Get someone else to blow your horn and the sound will carry twice as far."

– Will Rogers

Mentors serve as role models, providing emotional support, feedback on how to improve, and other advice. They can sit at any level in the hierarchy as long as they're positioned to help others understand and navigate corporate politics. By focusing on a protégé's personal and professional development, a mentor increases the other's sense of competence and self-worth.

Sponsors, on the other hand, are senior executives with influence; they have the power to promote careers. The goal of the sponsor is to make sure that promising people are considered for challenging assignments and advancement opportunities. As advocates, they go beyond giving feedback and advice: they help a protégé gain visibility in the company. They fight to get their protégés to the next level.

Mentors and sponsors whether they're personal (such as an executive parent), professional (a good boss or colleague), or social (friends through associations, volunteer works, or other community activities) enhance your career. The best of them are good listeners and communicators, well-informed about companies and industries, and empathetic to the needs of others.

In its report, "Fulfilling the Promise: How More Women on Corporate Boards Would Make America and American Companies More Competitive," the Committee for Economic Development says mentoring should be a priority of corporate executives: "The development of talent within an organization is critical to long-term competitiveness ... We challenge senior executives, men in particular, to take responsibility for developing, grooming, and advocating for talented women within their companies. This means giving such women the experiences necessary to become effective board members."

Maggie Wilderotter took advice like that to heart when she began a program that matches each of her top lieutenants with a board member for at least two years of informal coaching. Executives improve their leadership ability and board ties. Directors get in-depth looks at possible future occupants of the corner office. At the time, she said she wanted board members to get to know her seven highest deputies "in a more meaningful way."

Is the chemistry good? Making the connection to a mentor or sponsor

Women who receive mentoring fare significantly better than their un-mentored counter parts. Studies have shown that: 1) more women than men report having mentors, 2) women's mentors typically have less organizational clout, and 3) women generally report greater benefit from the psychological and social aspects of mentoring than men do.

But which mentor or sponsor is better a man or a woman? Generally speaking, women provide more role modeling and less career development, while men offer less psychological support and more career advancement. Senior women may be afraid that junior women will be too dependent and that they will expect them to be perfect. Junior women may be afraid that they may be overpowered by a senior woman or be disappointed when their dependency needs are not met.

"Early in my career, I didn't appreciate the importance of mentors and sponsors — I always assumed that my work would speak for itself. Well, that is just not reality. Excellent performance is just the entry point."

the late **Fritzi Woods** | a former director of Jamba Juice and Ignite Restaurants

ACTION STEPS

Picking a person to be your mentor is like starting any relationship:

First, find out what potential mentors stand for: Google them, read their books and speeches, and talk to mutual friends and colleagues, especially those who have worked with the person.

Second, discover a commonality with the one who interests you the most: a personal bond is the glue for a business mentoring relationship.

Third, make a good impression. The secret to that is performance: the protégé's obligation in the relationship is to "deliver the goods" as promised.

> " An ounce
> of
> performance
> is worth pounds
> of promises. "

– Mae West

Being asked to join a board is not a happenstance event. It's what comes of decades of excellent work — work that advances not just a career but a bias for action and a passion for meaningful outcomes. In your pursuit of a board position, you're living the words of Antoine de Saint-Exupery: "True happiness comes from the joy of deeds well done, the zest of creating things new." This section includes ideas for achieving success by sharpening qualities you already have.

"You were not chosen randomly: no one is on a board only because she was lucky to be in the right place at the right time. You are there because you have value to give, and you were selected because of that value even if you think you don't have the qualifications. So, be confident in your own worth and your own knowledge."

Yolanda Auza
an entrepreneur of Librerias Wilborada 1047, an advisory board member of Engineering School Universidad de los Andes and WCD, and co-chair of WCD Colombia Chapter

CONTRIBUTING FROM "DAY ONE"

THE GIRL SCOUTS WERE (AND ARE) RIGHT

"The Girl Scout motto is 'Be prepared.' In the 1947 Girl Scout Handbook, the motto was explained this way: 'A Girl Scout is ready to help out wherever she is needed. Willingness to serve is not enough; you must know how to do the job well, even in an emergency.' The Girl Scout slogan, in use since 1912, is 'Do a good turn daily.' The slogan is a reminder of the many ways girls can contribute positively to the lives of others."

– The Girl Scouts Organization

Getting ready to serve on a board begins with one's own career performance and planning; but it doesn't stop there. Success as a board member starts from the day you get an invitation to join.

Here are tips for doing a good job as a director, from day one:

Know the company and industry

Come to your first board meeting with a solid understanding of the company, its history, culture, and strategy. Background research will help you identify how you'll add value as a board member, while winning the respect of fellow board members.

Spend time on the company's website where you'll find annual reports and SEC filings which will give you insights into the company's financials, markets for its securities, any current or recently settled legislation, management's discussion and analysis, and internal controls and disclosure certifications. The financial statements especially will tell you if the company's revenues are increasing, decreasing, or flat; if the company is generating positive earnings or losses; and if cash flows and general liquidity are adequate.

Read the press releases on the site, and then use search engines to find current and past media coverage, articles, and blogs. Is the company a leader in its industry? Is there buzz about its future, maybe an anticipated sale, takeover, or turnaround?

Learn about the company's products and services to better understand the changes that have been made to strategy over time. Know the company's strengths and weaknesses, as well as trends affecting its competitors, including start ups introducing potentially game-changing products.

"Before interviewing for a board and long before a first board meeting, I try to learn all about current issues for the industry, the competition, the company's products, its customers — everything," says Jan Babiak. "It's not because when I walk into the boardroom anyone will expect me to know these things   indeed, board colleagues have said to me, 'We don't expect a lot from any board member in the first year, but we were really surprised because you made a contribution right from the beginning.' I can tell you, that's not because I'm smarter than anyone else, probably not even close; it's because I do a lot of research. That's gives me confidence so that I don't feel so much like a fish out of water on the first day."

Learn how the board works

Do all you can in advance to find out about how the board operates, about its governance system, the lead director, any possible committee openings, and each committee's focus. What skills do the other directors bring to the table and what skills does the board need? Ask the nominating committee chair to recommend an educational program. Also take these "above and beyond " steps:

Ask for minutes of past board meetings; they'll give you insight into the focus or discussion and the decision-making process. Teresa Ressel, former CEO of UBS Securities and a director of ON Semiconductor Corp, says that historical minutes "keep one from falling into a 'flavor of the month' framework. Perspective can help you keep an open mind and stay focused on the right things."

Attend audit committee meetings (even if you're not on the committee) to gain a greater understanding of the financials and the risk management oversight process.

During the interview process, ask "What keeps you up at night?" The answer can tell you a lot about the company and about the board.

Do your homework

Your board-specific research should focus on two questions: What gaps is the board trying to fill? What contribution can you make given your specific background and skills?

What is the company's turnover? If employees are leaving in droves or staying for many years, find out why. High turnover could indicate an extremely competitive war for talent in the industry or an unpleasant work environment. Low attrition could signal that the company is a great place to work or simply be the consequence of a very soft job market. To dig deeper, find out how employees feel about the company. Ask for the company's employee survey results. The surveys typically measure attitudes about the company's ethics, strategy, and long-term growth. Either way, as business leaders we know that highly satisfied and engaged people are essential to the health and success of a business.

Before the first board meeting (if possible) or during your first year, introduce yourself to management and to the other directors. Establish relationships with the CEO and CFO and other key executives, such as general counsel, head of HR, chief operating officer, and CIO. Continue to meet individually on a regular basis, since these meetings will give you insight into strategy and concerns. But don't form tight relationships immediately. Pick up on non-verbal signals in the room to understand the dynamics. Find what you have in common with others and understand the skills and perspectives you bring to the table.

Spend time visiting different parts or divisions of the company. Depending on the business, visit stores, plants and factories, and offices/sites outside the country. Seeing these locations and meeting people outside the C-suite will teach you about the company's culture and operations.

Of course, there's also homework for each board meeting: a great deal of background is sent in advance. Read it carefully so you don't ask questions that are already covered in the materials. As you're learning about the company, ask management (particularly the CFO) questions before a meeting. Use board dinners or executive sessions to ask the other directors about specific topics (Have they been addressed? What was the outcome?).

KPMG's Kathy Hopinkah Hannan offers this advice: "You have to do your homework—that's being authentic. If you know the industry, understand the landscape, and ask probing questions, you'll get respect. You have to be a systemic thinker. How does everything connect? Connecting the dots is really important."

"First and most important, you need to construct an orientation: Take control of the process! Don't just take what's given to you, but immerse yourself in other information that's out there on the company and on its competitive landscape. Talk to management and board members to get their perspectives on what's important."

Eleanor Bloxham | CEO of The Value Alliance and Corporate Governance Alliance and co-chair of WCD Columbus Chapter

ACTION TIPS

At your first meeting, do the following:

If there are no name plates, ask where you should sit.

Study the bios of the board members. Find one thing in common or something that interests you (not related to the board) for your first casual conversation.

Use a journal to write thoughts and questions. Some questions are best left unasked until you're up the learning curve a bit. List them and get back to them later, or use them to develop relationships with other board members and management after the meetings or at breaks.

Make note of how board members interact. Draw the table in your journal and put everyone's name in place so you can remember their names, faces, and each one's opinions when you review your notes.

NOTHING VENTURED, NOTHING GAINED

"You've got to jump off cliffs all the time and build your wings on the way down."

– Ray Bradbury

Alison Winter suggests that women wanting to serve on a board get out of their comfort zones: "When you step up and do something that's hard or new, you'll learn something. Being well prepared includes taking some personal risks. My first board meeting was tough. I wasn't young really — I was over 40 — but I still felt young and small in experience. The guys in the room are big shots, people who are in the paper every day, people who are running corporations. You've got to be at least a little brave! And not be afraid to learn. You do have value to contribute: Take the chances you're given."

Martha Finn Brooks, retired President and COO of Novelis, Inc. and a director of Bombardier, Jabil, Inc., and Algeco Scotsman, recalls the role that risk-taking played in her success: "At one point in my career, I chose to go with a new company that was spun off from an established one. In this way, I gained experience building a corporate structure and a new board of directors, honed my skills in dealing with Wall Street, and got to develop a new culture in a new enterprise. After a difficult start and a few mistakes, I got my chance to lead the company."

My First Board — MERLE OKAWARA

"When I took my own company public, that was my first board — it didn't prepare me for joining other boards, obviously! The first board I was appointed to as an outsider was Avon Japan. I was speaking at a conference, and the president of Avon, an American man, asked me if I would like to join the board. Of course, I was flabbergasted, but I went after this opportunity with great enthusiasm.

"The first board experience can be very intimidating, for men as well as for women. You have to do your homework. You have to know about the company, about the dynamics of its board, and about the issues in the industry, so that you feel a bit more comfortable. Usually, when a woman enters the room, it is full of middle-aged men in black suits, so the first meeting can be awkward. It's important to look professional and to act like we belong at the table."

DEMYSTIFY THE OTHER BOARD MEMBERS

"Get to know the chef and you will start to enjoy dining out even more."

— John Walters

Yolanda Auza urges new board members not to be intimidated: "You see these 'big personalities' at the table and think you have to do or say something fantastic just to be in the same room. But soon enough, you realize: they're people just like you. They have experiences to share, but so do you — everyone is just human! The key to being happy and productive on a board is that you all respect each other."

Sherry Barrat suggests telling it like it is: "I've never been afraid of asking for help. Pick someone — I got to know the two men who sat on both sides of me at the table — and say, 'This is my first corporate board: can you help me understand more about the industry, the company, the regulatory environment, and the board's work?' This isn't being weak; it's being honest. People like that."

Cathy Allen, agrees: "Before I even get to a first meeting, I talk to every single board member, as well as the general counsel and the senior executives in the company. I want to know not just how the company operates, but also the politics of the board, so that I'll have a sense of who people are and how they coalesce. Then, during that first board meeting, it's best not to say a lot; rather, listen and watch the body language and interactions among directors. By the second meeting, you're ready to participate because you understand the board on three levels: intellectual (what's being talking about), emotional level (what are the hotspots or issues), and interest (who's really engaged)."

"Women don't get to the board room easily; we get there after a career of putting tough issues on the table. But typically, we're not part of 'the club': we're newcomers all the time, and we survive by our charm (if we're blessed with that) and, more importantly, by our wit and grit. When you walk into that room as a woman, you're naturally doing what you've always done."

Donna James | Managing Director of Lardon & Associates, LLC and director of L Brands, Time Warner Cable, Marathon Petroleum Corporation, and FIS Group, addressing the first annual WCD Global Institute

WHEN TO TALK, WHAT TO SAY

"Courage is what it takes to stand up and speak; courage is also what it takes to sit down and listen."

– Winston Churchill

The right words, at the right time, are powerful. But when it comes to speaking up in a board meeting, it's often best to take it easy in the beginning.

Find the balance between being in the game and being a team player. Don't be afraid to ask thought-provoking questions — questions that further your understanding of the subject matter   but don't be the director who comments on everything. Be strong enough to have a point of view, but understand that you are part of a group of individuals who govern together.

Evelyn Dilsaver, a director of Aeropostale, Tempur Sealy, and Blue Shield of California and an advisory board member of Protiviti, offers this advice: "When you are a new director entering the boardroom for the first time, it is important to listen, really listen to the other directors, to management, and to mid-level management, so that you have a sense of the strengths of the company. When it's your turn to speak, ask yourself 'What's missing in the discussion? Where will my perspective add value?'"

ACTION TIPS

Here are five tips for finding your voice:

Be authentic.

Find out why you were selected for the board so you can deliver on that value proposition.

Don't sell yourself short. Remember, you have the skills and knowledge that have earned you the right to be at the table.

Be a good listener and observer. Use the first few board meetings to get the "tempo" of the board and the measure of each individual director's strengths.

On the other hand, have the courage of your convictions. As a director, you are obligated to discuss different points of view to help move the board forward together to reach effective decisions.

The late Fritzi Woods liked to talk about the value of being quiet, at least during the first few meetings as a new board member: "There's no 'cookie cutter' timeframe for talking at a board meeting. Often, what works is determined by the culture of that board. I've been on boards where just a few people dominate, period. And I've been in environments where other people's ideas are either dismissed or appropriated by the dominant member. On some boards, there's a lot of discussion in the room; in others, there's a lot of discussion pre-in-the-room, so if you're not getting in on that discussion, you're kind of lost. That's the part that can be scary. But on any and every board there comes a time when you have to have a point of view."

Woods suggested these questions for first-time directors.

Outside the room, ask other directors questions like these:
- What is the board doing that's really effective, and what's not worth your time?
- What skillsets do you think the board needs?
- Is there anything about the company's strategies that concerns you?
- What are we not spending enough time on?

After a presentation, ask the speaker questions like these:
- What questions should we have asked that you would like to address?
- What part of your presentation needed extra time and work to prepare?

When the timing is right in a meeting, ask questions like these:
- What are our key assumptions about this business strategy?
- How does our governance enable better operations, risk management, and regulatory compliance?

Speaking at the first annual WCD Global Institute, Kyung Yoon, encouraged women to change the dynamic of the discussion around the table: "Sometimes, directors get used to just agreeing with the chairman. Responses and relationships get baked in. But women are typically coming from the outside, or they're more recently on the board. So, they don't make assumptions. Many times, a woman can raise her hand and say, 'We need to talk about this some more, or how about some more facts, or have you thought about this?' That's a better way to get things done."

"I am a much better leader because I had three kids — they don't do what you want them to do when you want them to do it. Organizations don't necessarily, either. You've got to listen. You've got to learn how to influence."

Ellen J. Kullman | CEO of DuPont (the first woman to lead the 208-year-old company), as quoted in Bloomberg Businessweek

WE TALK TO A DIVERSITY CHAMPION: CHARLES "CHAD" HOLLIDAY, JR.

Chad Holliday is retired Chair and CEO of DuPont, a director of Deere & Co., Royal Dutch Shell, and CH2MHILL and chair of Bank of America. Since 2007, Holliday has served as a director at Deere & Co., He is Chairman Emeritus of Catalyst, a nonprofit organization dedicated to expanding opportunities for women, and Chairman Emeritus of the board of the US Council on Competitiveness, a nonpartisan, nongovernmental organization working to ensure US prosperity.

› Why does diversity matter?

"Using the talent — the right talent — of the whole workforce is central to a company's competitive advantage. In fact, rating agencies should make diversity a key issue. Now, as big boards are using search firms to show there's no bias in selection, these firms need to look at new candidates. At the same time, more networking among women on boards is helpful. And serving on major non-profit boards can provide good experience."

› What advice would you give to women directors?

"First, you need to focus on culture. The way you look at a culture of a company is to look at its totems, what it holds up to high esteem and taboos, what it's against.

"Second, you've got to ask a lot of questions. Ask probing questions, ask follow on questions, ask why. Ask astute questions that help the management think about perspectives important to the business. But don't try to operate the company. Put your nose in; keep your fingers out — that's the line between board members and management. If you're not happy with how the company is being run, change the management.

"Third, we're in a different world today. If you're sitting around waiting for the economy to return to what it was, you're going to wait a very, very long time. So, I believe that management and boards need to look at the new realities, look at the growth rates, look at the sustainable resources that are available to us, look at which countries are going to grow more rapidly in this period of time and which have aging populations which will slow them down. How do we put all that together to find opportunities? With seven billion people that need to be served, there are a lot of opportunities in the world. It's just up to us to find them, and I think women directors can be a great contributor to that."

My First Board — DEBORAH WINCE-SMITH

"Before I joined my first board, I wished I'd known that a board doesn't need to operate in unison. But the members do need to have a synergy of knowledge and expertise. That's why diversity is so important. If everyone comes out of finance, or technology, or M&A, or a certain industrial sector — or if everyone is of the same gender, race, or age — the board's perspective will be very limited, which is a liability in today's world, where companies deal with unprecedented complexity and global challenges.

"In my first board experience, I learned several important lessons. Take advantage of the orientation programs that the company offers. Make sure you have the opportunity to visit the headquarters, meet a number of the executive team players, and get to know your fellow board members in a relaxed, social setting before your first meeting. Don't be pigeonholed. You have to be somebody who can look across the whole spectrum of challenges and, to do that, you have to step outside of your comfort zone."

KEEP YOUR EYE ON THE BALL

"Concentrate all your thoughts upon the work at hand. The sun's rays do not burn until brought to a focus."

— Alexander Graham Bell

One of the first steps you should take as a new board member is to learn all the board processes and board reporting systems. Larger companies will have board training: if your company does not, find an organization such as a university or an association that offers it. If you are on the board of a larger company, you can expect to get a "board book" of information at least one week in advance of the board meeting that outlines each issue that will be discussed by the board.

According to Melissa Means it's a good idea to have access to the board/committee calendar to identify key dates and meetings throughout the year and plan/prepare accordingly. She also suggests meeting with the board's outside advisers (such as auditors and compensation consultants) as they can help with training and education, while also providing some history (how did we get here? where did we come from?).

You'll want to know your board participation requirements and expected behaviors, committee structure, the backgrounds and roles of other directors, company bylaws, as well as its business plans, financials, and pending risks (especially any litigation). Depending on your country or locality, there may be laws governing the legal responsibilities of the board. Get to know these: the penalties for non-compliance can be high. Ask penetrating questions: dig under the surface. Then, you'll be fulfilling your obligation as an independent board member.

Also, as a new member on the board, you should ask for a list of key ethical and risk issues facing the organization. You may also want to meet with the general counsel or chief compliance officer, if your company has one. Your intent should be to gain a deep understanding of the company's internal controls and risks. "Our understanding of risk needs to expand continuously," says Wendy Luhabe. "Risk assessment and management need be part of a very dynamic, very flexible process, no longer confined to what we traditionally call risk."

In the current economic and geopolitical environment, your board should raise questions like these:

- Do we have an effective enterprise risk management system? Would a coup or leadership change in another country impact our supply chain? Do we have effective business continuity plans in place to deal with the impact of natural disasters?
- How would we deal with a hostile bid? What if a potential merger or takeover bid fails?
- How could actions by employees harm our reputation? Are outside activists interested in harming our business? How secure is our enterprise systems against hackers/cyber-terrorism?
- What is the company's social media strategy/policy?
- How vulnerable are our products to tampering? In production, do we have the right quality controls in place?
- How do we imagine the unimaginable?

The WCD/Groysberg/Heidrick & Struggles *2012 Board of Directors Survey* captures the opinions of more than 1,000 directors from around the world. Here's what they said about the issues facing today's boards:

External issues: When asked to name the political issues most relevant to their role as corporate board directors, both men and women cited "unemployment/the economy" and "the federal budget deficit" as the top two. After that, the genders diverge slightly, with women citing "healthcare costs" and men naming "energy costs" as third.

Regulation: The threat of more regulation is seen as the biggest obstacle to achieving strategic objectives, according to both men and women US directors. A close second: the need to "attract and retain top talent." Directors outside the US ranked regulatory environment and talent concerns equally. "Despite the good intentions behind regulatory reform, board directors do not see increased governance regulation as the answer to the economic crisis," says Alison Winter.

Strategy: A core board responsibility is oversight of corporate strategy, since that drives long-term value for shareholders. As a new board member, you should take these steps:

- Request a detailed briefing of current strategies.
- Ask for an analysis of trends affecting the company's industry and its markets, as well as the economy and political environment as a whole. Then, evaluate the strategy through those filters.

"Companies and countries start behaving — acting and planning — in a different way. Why? Because of population growth, climate change, urbanization, resource scarcity, and increasing unemployment. We have to worry about these things. If a company does not include various stakeholders in its strategic dialogues, the risks are huge. The new board member has to have a long-term view."

Usha Rao-Monari | a director and CEO of Global Water Development Partners, a Blackstone Portfolio Company

WE TALK TO A DIVERSITY CHAMPION: BORIS GROYSBERG

Boris Groysberg, PhD, Richard P. Chapman Professor of Business Administration at the Harvard Business School, lead the analysis of the data from the WCD/Groysberg/Heidrick & Struggles *2012 Board of Directors Survey*. Here, he answers questions about the survey's most salient findings. Many of these insights can also be found in the *Harvard Business Review* articles "Dysfunction in the Boardroom" and "Talent Management: Boards Give Their Companies an 'F'" by Boris Groysberg, PhD, and Deborah Bell.

> **If you had to name the three most striking findings from the 2012 survey, what would they be?**

"First, women have to be more qualified than men to be considered for boards. Contrary to popular belief, female directors have more operational and leadership experience than male directors. Second, boards don't know how to leverage diversity. The women we surveyed said they were not treated as full members of the group, though the men were largely oblivious to this problem. Third, great talent is not enough to create a great board. Boards need processes and cultures that encourage inclusiveness as well as diversity."

> **Can these shortfalls be reversed?**

"Let's just look at the challenges in recognizing and leveraging the talents of women.

"Corporate directors say talent management is their single greatest strategic challenge, but the vast majority of directors say their organizations are not doing a good job of that. In fact, in two practices in particular — 'firing' and 'leveraging diversity' — many companies fail dismally. I think that's because many boards still rely on their own, mostly white, mostly male, networks to fill seats. Our research suggests they'd do a better job if they had objective processes for selecting members based on the skills and attributes that boards need to be effective."

› How about a word to the wise?

"Don't be surprised if you run into obstacles. Even after you're invited to join a board, you might find the reception to be cool. Diversity is counting the numbers; inclusiveness is making the numbers count.

"During my research, I heard this story: A successful, accomplished woman in financial services was asked to join the board of a multibillion-dollar public company. She was its first and, for many years, only woman director. She brought needed financial expertise to the board, as well as a deep understanding of the company's industry; yet she routinely felt shut out. During board meetings, her questions were greeted not with respect, but as intrusions into the 'real' conversation among the men. In fact, the chairman had taken her aside many times and asked her to be 'less vocal' and to 'stop arguing her point' during meetings. She recalled once when she was pursuing a question about a strategic decision when a male director interrupted her and exclaimed, 'You're behaving just like my daughter! You're arguing too much—just stop.'

"The antidotes for that kind of prejudice include: team-building training for members, developing and promoting diversity at every level of the organization, and establishing a culture of accountability and responsibility."

BOARD WORK IS A TEAM SPORT

"Talent wins games, but teamwork and intelligence win championships."

– Michael Jordan

The best leadership comes from teams whose members are bound by mutual respect, a commitment to the future value of the company, and strong bonds of trust. Great boards support smart risk taking with prudent oversight, wise counsel, and encouragement. The right kind of collaboration is an asset beyond measure. For the new board member, this means two things:

Be in the game: Don't be afraid to ask thought provoking questions. It's important that you establish your ability to contribute early on. And remember, there are no "dumb" questions – it is the responsibility of the board directors to express and discuss different points of view to help move the board forward together to reach effective decisions. That is the art of being an effective board member.

Be a team player: Don't be the director who continuously asks questions or comments on everything. Be strong enough to contribute, have a point of view, but understand that you are part of a group of individuals who govern together. Be respectful of cultural differences. Directors need to be able to disagree without being disagreeable, and be likeable without trying to be liked.

While speaking at the third annual WCD Global Institute, Ann Dunwoody drew on her experience as the first four-star general in the US Army (now retired) and as a director of L3, LMI Logistics Management Institute, Republic Services Group and Council of Trustees Association of United States Army, to offer this advice to women serving on boards: "Communicate, collaborate, and cooperate. You're not the only player on the field. The more you can reach out to share, to talk, to communicate, and to make others understand and appreciate the importance of your role in accomplishing a mission — and if everyone knows they're vital — there's really nothing you can't do. In the old days, information was power. Now, the real power is *shared* information: that's what helps us be successful."

Shirley Ann Jackson, PhD, agrees and offers these tips:

"First, stay focused on corporate strategy and good governance, capital allocation around the strategy, legal and regulatory issues.

"Second, never be afraid to ask questions, even if they are definitional, because one can make an assumption that is mistaken (for example, that everyone sitting around the table knows the meaning of an acronym). It is important to ask questions about strategy and governance, to have the opportunity to talk with other executives in the company (not just the CEO); and to get to know the up-and-comers, the next generation, because many of them are people the board will make decisions about in the future.

"Third, spend the time with fellow board members and learn from them."

"Before the annual evaluation comes along, ask other board members for their open, honest feedback on your performance. It's great to do this early on so that you know that you are fitting in to the chemistry of the board, that you are not rubbing people the wrong way, and that you are creating effective relationships with everyone on the board."

Eleanor Bloxham | CEO of The Value Alliance and Corporate Governance Alliance and co-chair of WCD Columbus Chapter

LEARNING NEVER STOPS

"He who asks a question is a fool for five minutes; he who does not remains a fool forever."

– Chinese proverb

No one is expected to have all of the answers to all the questions all the time. In her remarks at the launching of the WCD Gulf Cooperative Council Chapter in Abu Dhabi, Martha Finn Brooks urged women directors to be direct and honest: "Leaders value others who aren't afraid to speak up." She also offered up these tips:

Don't be afraid of disagreement, and don't take it as a personal insult. A disagreement is an invitation to understand someone else's perspective, and it's an opportunity to learn.

Challenge *and* support management. Your success starts with the selection of the company to join as a director. Look for a company where your experience will be relevant and useful, but where you'll still learn new things.

Avoid boards that are for show. If the CEO wants to control all the information given to the board, allows little time for discussion, and dislikes being challenged, the board can't add value to the governance process.

Find small ways to interface with the company beyond the board room. Set your computer to do a Google Alert on the company's name and industry so you can pick up all press coverage and blogs on the company, both positive and negative. The more you can learn about the company and the industry, the more valuable you'll be as a director.

Develop trusted relationships with a few other directors, so you can test your ideas outside the boardroom. If the ideas are worth pursuing, you'll speak with more confidence and are more likely to get support from the rest of the board.

"I treat each new board like a foreign-service assignment. I consider it a huge learning experience. The fact that I learn something at every meeting is one of the reasons that I enjoy serving on boards. I've heard it said that serving on boards is like flying an airplane: utterly boring for about 95 percent of the time, and then terrorizing. You really have to focus. Before joining a board, I read up on the other directors so I'll know who they are and where they come from — when I was in the Foreign Service, I did the same thing before meeting with a Minister or Head of State"

Frances Cook | former Ambassador to Oman and to the Republic of Cameroon, a former director at Arlington Associates Limited, and former chair of Lonrho PLV and the Ballard Group

"We are drowning in information, while starving for wisdom. The world henceforth will be run by synthesizers, people able to put together the right information at the right time, think critically about it, and make important choices wisely. "

– E. O. Wilson

Your success as a director depends on what you know — about the company and its business, about the industry and its future, and about the changing world. Take to heart the philosophy of Albert Einstein: "You have to learn the rules of the game. And then you have to play better than anyone else." This section contains practical information about how a board gets things done.

"Over almost 30 years of involvement with large public companies, I am seeing directors get much more engaged with the job. Boards are carefully building a diverse set of skills and experiences among their members, and they're increasingly less likely to pick only friends to join them. These are healthy changes."

Martha Finn Brooks
retired President and COO of Novelis, Inc. and a director of Bombardier, Jabil, Inc., and Algeco Scotsman

BOARD WORK

GETTING THINGS DONE

"Productivity is never an accident. It is always the result of a commitment to excellence, intelligent planning, and focused effort."
— Paul J. Meyer

A board of directors has a heavy work load, and in the best boards, directors bring diverse expertise to the task of governance. The way things get done — efficiently and effectively — is through committees and special advisory boards. In fact, in the article "5 Fresh Ideas for Getting More from Boards," *Boardroom INSIDER* says that committees do more than the work of the board, they're also a tool for better governance: "Committees are the ideal bodies for technical, compliance and box-ticking stuff. Smart, active … committees should handle the great majority of compliance matters, and deliver neatly-wrapped reports and recommendation to the full board for approval. This gives the full board more time for discussion on big topics. If your board spends more than a few minutes picking apart a committee's work, either the committee is underperforming or the board is too tangled in minutiae."

Here is an overview of the roles and responsibilities of committees, some traditional, some emerging:

[handwritten: Most time Consuming on average, 8 times/year, 3 hours @ a time]

AUDIT COMMITTEE

The audit committee is charged with oversight of financial reporting and disclosure. The SEC and NASDAQ prescribe that an audit committee have at least

*[handwritten: * Great to listen in]*

three directors who are independent (that is, they do not receive any compensation from the company other than director fees), and financially literate (that is, they understand the financial reporting issues and complexities related to the company's business activities). If you've ever worked in accounting or finance, you could be an ideal candidate for the audit committee. But even if you're not on the committee, you should attend some meetings to gain a better understanding of the company.

Stakeholders — investors, capital markets, and regulators — want assurance that the financial statements of public companies are accurate and transparent. Various regulations, such as the Sarbanes-Oxley Act, specify responsibilities for audit committees, including oversight of financial reporting and internal controls, of external and internal audits (the audit committee selects, compensates, oversees, and evaluates the external auditor), and of risk management.

According to KPMG's essay titled "Audit Committee Priorities for 2013" featured in the "Governance Challenges 2013 and Beyond" report by the National Association of Corporate Directors, the agenda for the audit committees is being shaped by economic uncertainty, globalization, digitization, and government regulation. For this reason, it's more important than ever that an audit committee be focused, yet flexible, to discern those issues that are on a critical path. Recognizing that priorities will vary by company and industry, KPMG suggests these priorities for the audit committee:

Stay focused on job #1: Financial accounting and reporting and internal controls

The challenges of global economic conditions, coupled with the impact of major public policy initiatives — deficit reduction and tax reform, healthcare, financial services regulation, new accounting standards, and a challenging regulatory environment — require the attention of every audit committee. The committees should 1) monitor fair value estimates, impairments, and management's assumptions underlying critical accounting estimates, and 2) consider how the disclosures can be improved to tell the company's story. Are *all* financial communications, including earnings releases and analyst calls, consistent with what is being said in the quarterly and annual filings? Recognizing that financial reporting quality starts with the CFO and finance organization, directors should maintain a sharp focus on management's financial reporting processes, making sure that they have the resources to succeed.

Reinforce audit quality and set clear expectations for the external auditor

Audit quality is enhanced when the audit committee 1) sets clear expectations for the external auditor, and 2) monitors auditor performance through frequent, quality communications and a rigorous assessment process. In selecting an external auditor, the committee should ask: "What is your proof of independence, objectivity, and skepticism? How does your internal system of quality control operate? How deep is your experience in auditing companies of like size and industry?" When evaluating a potential auditor, the committee should meet the lead partner and other members of the audit team. Although regulations vary by country, committee members should understand how the auditor reaches its conclusions and be able to discuss any of its judgments.

Monitor the impact of the environment on the company's compliance programs

Internal audit is most effective when it's focused on the critical risks to the business, including key operational risks and related controls—not just compliance and financial reporting risks. What's changed in the operating environment? What are the risks posed by the extended organization—sourcing, outsourcing, and sales and distribution channels? The audit committee plays a role in setting clear expectations and making sure internal audit has the resources, skills, and expertise to succeed. One particular challenge   given today's complex supply chains, new technologies, and an ever tighter connection between growth opportunities and emerging markets   is an increasing vulnerability to fraud, misconduct, and compliance risk. The global regulatory environment is very complicated. The audit committee also has to monitor the regulatory compliance of its vendors in the global supply chain.

Understand the company's tax risks and how they're being managed

Oversight of tax risk is an increasingly important responsibility for audit committees, prompted largely by the complexity of operating in multiple tax regimes. Other pressures   including increased enforcement at all levels, demands for greater transparency and disclosure, potential business tax reform, and reputational risks   have also raised the stakes. To stay abreast of tax risks, the audit committee should establish clear communications with the CFO or Chief Tax Officer. Does the company have enough resources and expertise to manage global tax liabilities? The audit committee can also help maximize collaboration between internal and external auditors.

Looking beyond "core" areas of oversight, KPMG identifies other ways the audit committee can contribute to better overall governance practices:

Does the committee have the right composition and structure to provide effective risk oversight?

Many audit committees are responsible for the company's enterprise risk management process. Over the years (by design or default), many have also assumed responsibility for other major risks facing the company — such as risks posed by globalization, cybersecurity and information technology (IT) risks, and other operational risks, as well as legal and regulatory compliance. Given the substantial time commitment required for this work, the audit committee needs specialized expertise. Board and audit committee effectiveness and accountability hinge on honest self-reflection, meaningful board assessments, and continuing director education.

How are digitization and social media affecting the company's competitive landscape?

The staggering pace of technology change has steadily pushed IT risk higher on the audit committee's agenda. At the same time, boards have expanded their focus beyond "defensive" IT risks — such as data privacy and security, social media/brand reputation, and protection of intellectual property and non-public financial information — to consider the transformational impact of game-changing technologies such as the cloud, social media, mobile, and "big data." Is management making the most of new technologies? If the company doesn't have a technology committee, how can the audit committee help ensure that management understands the opportunities and risks posed by emerging technologies?

Does the company's leadership style and culture enforce a commitment to integrity?

Is the audit committee (and board) hearing views from those below senior management and outside the company? Are there dissenting views? Does the information coming from management, internal audit, and external auditors tell a consistent story?

Writing in *Directors & Boards*, K. Sue Redman, President of Redman Advisors LLC and Executive Professor of Texas A&M University, suggests that the way information is shared can improve the committee members' productivity and effectiveness:

First, ask committee members what information they want and how they want to receive it. This improves the relevance of the information provided.

Second, make sure the committee members work closely with the company's accounting and finance department to reduce the time required to review financial data and other information, increase overall effectiveness, and ensure that committee's actions comply with its legal duties of care and loyalty.

Third, consider segregating members of the audit committee into these categories: 1) members who are experienced but very busy and, therefore, wanting to spend a minimal amount of time fulfilling their financial oversight responsibility; 2) members who are not interested in or knowledgeable of the technical accounting and financial environment, but have an expertise (such as technology or risk management) that's valuable to the committee and the board; and 3) members who understand detailed accounting and financial reporting (the "audit committee financial expert"). Once the members have been grouped, it's easier to customize the structure and content of the audit committee packages.

In *Boardroom INSIDER*, Ralph Ward, Publisher of *Boardroom INSIDER*, editor of *The Corporate Board* magazine and author of *Boardroom Q&A*, suggests one more audit committee agenda item that would make the members' job easier and more effective: career development for the CFO. " Though audit committees depend on building a strong, open relationship with the CFO, they've done little when it comes to hiring, evaluation and succession planning for the role. A KPMG Audit Committee Institute survey found that just 40 percent of committee respondents say their company has a CFO succession plan in place (no fair asking how many committees don't know one way or the other). What can the committee do to make this process more effective from end to end?"

Ward recommends building a strong relationship with the current CFO as the first step, while asking these questions: "How much discussion time does your audit committee chair spend pre-meeting with the CFO? How much time does your CFO spend sitting in at committee meetings? Does the committee chair become involved in the job evaluation process for the CFO, and to what level? Does the full board as well as the audit committee offer evaluation input? How much input does the board have in setting CFO performance goals and measures? How does the board's evaluation of the CFO tie in with the metrics used for the CEO?" Today's audit committee is fully informed and fully engaged.

My First Board — SHIRLEY ANN JACKSON, PhD

"Thirty years ago, I was doing research in theoretical physics at Bell Telephone Labs. But I also was involved with the state of New Jersey in areas having to do with science, technology, and public policy. One day, I was told by a colleague at AT&T that the CEO of New Jersey Resources wanted to talk to me about the possibility of joining that company's board. A few weeks later, I had lunch with the CEO, Jim Dolan. We had a great conversation, and he asked me to join the board.

"I had never been on a corporate board — the board of a publicly-traded company — so, right away I learned as much about the company as I could. Early on, I was asked to join the audit committee. In those days, the audit committee did not quite have the heft it has today, (since Sarbanes Oxley and so forth), but it was an excellent way to learn different aspects of the company. Later, I became chair of the audit committee and I remained as chair the whole time that I was on the board — for 13 years.

"I think it is important for a new board member to be a student of strategy and governance — to be observant, to serve wholeheartedly on committees, to try to be on different committees if one can do that, and to never be afraid to ask questions.

NOMINATING COMMITTEE *almost as much time as audit (8 times x 2 hrs)*

The nominating committee selects and presents candidates for office within the organization. Its members have the power to bring more traditional boards into today's realities by supporting a multinational, multicultural approach to governance.

In the *Financial Times* article, "Skills that Every Nom-Gov Committee Needs Today," Jill Kanin-Lovers, a director of Heidrick & Struggles, Dot Foods, and Homeownership, and an advisory board member of WCD, asks "What qualities should a nominating and governance committee look for when assessing itself and recruiting new members?" Her answers suggest behavior for any director considering a role on the nominating committee:

Understand the "surgical strike" that's needed for the company

The nominating committee needs to identify director candidates who can contribute directly to the strategic needs of the business. Today, well-rounded directors are often less valuable than candidates with specific experiences, such as launching a digital business approach or helping a company expand globally. At the same time, the committee needs to assess the cultural fit of a candidate with the board and the company. Ultimately, all the expertise in the world cannot compensate for a dysfunctional working relationship with other board members.

Get out in front of shareholder irritants

Proxy advisory firms give annual report cards on corporate governance. Therefore, a nominating committee needs to understand shareholder issues early on to enable effective communication with shareholders about the hot-button issues driving their concerns. The committee has to keep directors current with new regulations that affect governance. Also, in this environment, it's increasingly important for directors to stay on top of issues, such as succession planning, by having qualified candidates who can replace a CEO if he or she resigned unexpectedly.

Lay it on the line

One task that is too frequently avoided is assessing the skills of current board members and determining when it is time for certain ones to move on. Nominating committees that run director evaluations through skill matrices or competency models may not win a popularity contest, but these measures are necessary for maintaining board excellence. Best practices demand candid assessments of directors and exactly how each one contributes to a company's governance.

Find under-the-radar candidates

CEOs make great candidates for board service, but limiting a search to CEOs means missing the breadth and depth of skills required by boards today. Beyond the corporate top spot are numerous candidates whose direct operational expertise might be just what's needed in the boardroom for a company's next big move. Younger talent — who may not have had the time to move up the ranks into a CEO position — can contribute meaningfully by virtue of their immersion in digital technologies and media.

✳ Board Evaluation

A ROADMAP FOR DECISION-MAKERS
FROM THE WCD GLOBAL NOMINATING COMMISSION

The Global Nominating Commission is a task force of board nominating committee chairs and members, as well as CEOs, dedicated to building diverse boards and candidate slates. The Commission's goals are to help build diverse boards that are multi-gender, multi-skilled, multi-national, multi-ethnic, and multi-generational, and to empower more women directors to be placed onto nominating committees.

Here is the most recent version of a roadmap for achieving that vision:

1. Make board succession a top priority. *The Global Board of Directors Study* from WCD, Heidrick & Struggles, and Professor Boris Groysberg, PhD, of the Harvard Business School, found that board and CEO succession planning needs to be a top priority for corporate boards. Only 40 percent of respondents globally said that their boards had an effective succession planning process for directors. Directors can use renewed attention to succession to improve diverse representation in the boardroom.

2. Encourage nominating committees to require that director slates include diverse candidates. Look to the National Football League's "Rooney's Rule" in the US, which ensures that an African-American candidate is considered in each coach search. Ensure women candidates are in every search. Create awareness of diverse director candidate databases and additional networks.

3. Work with the CEO to champion diverse candidates in the pipelines and networks. Doug Conant at Campbell's Soup sponsored Denise Morrison; Chad Holliday at DuPont sponsored Ellen Kullman.

4. Connect diverse director candidates with board sponsors who can influence their board placement — especially for the candidate's "first appointment." Identify candidates through personal connections, word-of-mouth, or a search firm. Then, identify a champion on each board, dedicated to making

a diversity appointment and ensuring a cultural fit. Build success upon success.

5. Candidly assess current directors and their contribution to governance each year. Also address term and age limits, as currently dictated by best practice.

6. Instill a process to review multiple criteria for new board members. Look for diversity not only of gender and ethnicity, but also of geography, skillsets, industry background, and other experiences.

7. Look beyond CEOs and "well-rounded" directors for candidates with specific skills that can contribute directly to the strategic needs of the business. Such skills can include digital innovation, strategic talent, supply chain management, risk management, cyber security, manufacturing in China and/or India, and global branding.

8. Identify how younger candidates can add fresh thinking to the boardroom. These candidates can be found especially in industries such as media, music, travel, and retail, which have been transformed by digital and social media. Ethnic and gender diversity are often more easily found in younger directors.

9. Mentor first-term board members on director effectiveness, board culture, and priorities. Help to **ease** the transition and ensure the success of diverse members.

10. Assure the "cultural fit" of a candidate with the board and the company. Boards need candor, courage, and cohesion.

11. Commit to director education, staying current with all regulatory and governance developments.

12. Identify a wide range of board opportunities and sponsor qualified women

for them. These positions can include serving on advisory boards, as well as boards of major national state, and city commissions, pension funds, and treasuries.

13. Promote diversity by speaking at leadership, governance, and industry organizations and conferences. Forge alliances with organizations and research partners to expand networks and resources. It is incumbent that nominating and governance committee members are visible at the top meetings and forums where they have the opportunity to meet potential directors and identify talent.

14. Use the Global Nominating Commission's web resource. This is a "go to" guide to research, articles, databases, organizations, director education resources, and action steps around board diversity.

"Male, Pale, Stale"

COMPENSATION COMMITTEE , *Corporate & Development Committee*

The compensation committee, tasked with deciding the CEO's and executive officers' compensations, has been on the hot seat for the past few years. The public conversation about fairness, income discrepancies, and pay for performance has never been more vociferous. The role of the compensation committee, which includes determining a compensation philosophy, is core to the company's mission and the execution of its business strategies. As more stakeholders including investors, analysts, media, government, and rating agencies demand a say on pay, the decisions of the compensation committee will continue to be under scrutiny.

In its recent publication, *The 2013 Compensation Committee Agenda: Go Beyond*, Pearl Meyer & Partners says today's committees need to go "beyond best practices, beyond data, beyond check-the-box compliance, and beyond the obvious" because a well-tailored compensation strategy sends strong signals to employees and the marketplace about the company's goals, priorities, and vision. "Simply following the crowd minimizes the real impact that a differentiated compensation strategy can have on building a strong management team focused on achieving the company's business strategy," the report says.

In the essay, "Paying Executives for Driving Long-Term Success" published in "Governance Challenges 2013 and Beyond," a report from the National Association of Corporate Directors, the consultants with Pearl Meyer & Partners argue that the compensation committee needs to understand many, different factors, including competitive market practice, talent turnover in the company, management's ability to address current needs and meet future objectives, business and investment cycles, and the company's culture as it affects decision-making, risk taking, recognition and rewards, and team-versus-individual behaviors.

"The relationship of pay delivery to company performance should be paramount," they conclude. "In approaching the design of executive compensation programs, compensation committees should keep three goals paramount: properly calibrating realizable pay with actual performance, balancing short-term performance risk with long-term retention needs, and balancing line of sight objectives with accountability for total shareholder returns."

Melissa Means adds this final observation: "Because compensation is the hot topic of the day, more and more board members (including those not currently on the compensation committee) are very interested in understanding more about their company's compensation programs. In some cases, other board members now attend regularly-scheduled compensation committee meetings to garner more information."

(For more information on Executive Compensation, please read the 2014 WCD Thought Leadership Council Report. To download a PDF of this report, go to www.womencorporatedirectors.com and find the Thought Leadership Council page under "WCD Initiatives" or go to:
http://www.womencorporatedirectors.com/?page=_ThoughtLeadership.)

ADVISORY BOARDS

Advisory boards are made up of outside experts who bring niche skills or expertise to a company's and board's decision-making. Their advice is non-binding; they possess no legal or fiduciary responsibility, serve at the company's discretion, and are flexible in size, composition, and length of service. Coincidently, they're a great way for potential director candidates to make themselves known to board members. Here are five ways advisory boards bring value to a company:

Walking the walk An advisory board provides intellectual capital (what you know), social capital (who you know), and creative capital (a catalyst for new ideas). Members focus without distraction on specific issues of strategy and operations; they're a catalyst for change and progress.

Minimizing risk, while maximizing opportunity Advisory boards play an important role in risk oversight, as they help evaluate strategies, analyze trends, identify discrepancies between plans and practices, and address issues of importance. To provide a rich perspective, an advisory board (like a board of directors) should be diverse, with members of different backgrounds and ages. At the same time, advisory boards themselves are risk-free investments; they have no fiduciary or legal responsibilities, while their fees and terms are limited.

Staying ahead of the moment Advisory boards should have limited, well-defined missions. Often they're used to anticipate the future, from deciding on a location for a new plant to evaluating market expansion opportunities. Also, an advisory board can test a strategy's soundness.

Anticipating the next big thing This is especially true of technology advisory boards, which are being used by leaders in every industry to find, and exploit emerging technologies and channels.

Opening doors to new networks As companies become more global, an advisory board (made up of the right members) can provide a bigger perspective. Members can be on the ground in the United States, Europe, Asia, Latin America, the Middle East, and Africa providing the local point of view that's so valuable in doing business internationally.

These new types of advisory boards are becoming increasingly common in today's companies:

Technology Advisory Board

When it comes to technology, the appeal of advisory boards is that they allow companies to tap the insights of experienced, often highly priced young talent whom they might not be able to hire as employees young hotshots who really know what's going on.

The hottest technology topics today — the cloud, data analytics, social media and mobility — are often not well understood by board directors. In fact, when WCD surveyed the participants of its third annual Global Institute, 55 percent of the directors said their boards are not comfortable with social media. The consultants of Spencer Stuart argue that changes in capabilities and experience are becoming increasingly necessary in a fast-changing world. For example, for some organizations digitally-savvy directors can make a significant contribution to the board and the company's digital initiatives — in and out of the boardroom, as Spencer Stuart explains in their white paper, "Digital Expertise in the Boardroom":

"Outside of the boardroom, a digital expert can be a unique partner to the executive team, serving alternatively as a sounding board, a translator and, potentially, a coach. Digital directors may be asked to take on additional projects for the CEO, such as advising on acquisition targets or critical new hires, and frequently make introductions to cutting-edge digital and technology companies.

"In the boardroom, executives with the appropriate digital expertise can demystify digital, help management and the board clarify the specific digital forces impacting the business, and provide insight into the ways customer behavior is changing and other important trends — all of which can advance the broader board's understanding of the issues at play for the business. As a result, the executive team can spend less time educating the board and more time in strategic discussions."

Amanda Gerut, Senior Reporter at *Agenda*, seconds that argument in her *Agenda* article, "Tech-Savvy Advisory Boards Can Help Directors": "As social media and digital technology grow more and more integral to companies' strategic plans, boards and senior management have begun assembling advisory boards made up of some of the most sought-after and youngest technology executives in the field … For the most part, they are helping directors and executives figure out how social media should fit into their organizations in the future." At least 10 Fortune 50 companies have formed such boards during the past two years.

Clara Shih applauds that trend: "Today's customers are social, mobile, and digital. There are over one billion active users worldwide on Facebook alone, and we are seeing new social networking sites from Pinterest to Instagram emerging every day. Companies need to be where their customers are in order to remain relevant, competitive, and top of mind."

Myla Villanueva makes the case for understanding mobile technologies: "The last ten years have seen a dramatic change and impact of technology on companies across this region. For example, we're seeing a 100 percent rate of penetration of mobile technology in just a year or two. It is important as a board member to understand that this is the access point to our part of the world."

Social media is not just for marketing, but rather can play a significant role in recruiting talent (especially Millennials), gathering the competitive intelligence useful in R&D and product design, sending messages to investors and the marketplace at large, and protecting the enterprise from security threats, as written in the article, "Social Media Intelligence for Corporate Directors"published in *Strategic Mindshare* by Cynthia Cohen, Founder and President of Strategic Mindshare, a director of Equity One and Steiner Leisure Services, a trustee of the Committee for Economic Development, an advisory board member of AnswerLab, DigiWorksCorp, Sophelle, and WCD and co-chair of WCD New York Chapter. She suggests these questions for getting a grip on social media:

1. Does the company have written policies governing social media use and control over content, branding, and intellectual property (e.g. copyright infringement protection)?
2. Does the board have an annual overview presentation covering social media use, corporate reputation, and competitive positioning?
3. Are social media uses and guidelines included in disaster recovery plans for communications?
4. Can the organization act 24/7 if needed in response to unanticipated events or media attacks from outside groups?
5. Are all current and planned brand names protected on social media platforms?
6. How is the company using social media to communicate strategy and values to various stakeholders?

Of course, as important as they are, social media and mobile technologies are just part of the big picture. "Technology continues to be a game changer for all industries," says Cathy Allen "What is new is the velocity of change and the resulting ambiguity that challenge boards to understand which way to go."

CORPORATE DIRECTORS ARE CLUELESS ABOUT IT

In *CIO* magazine, Kim S. Nash, Managing Editor of *CIO Magazine*, writes that even as companies are relying more on technology to come up with innovative business models and fresh ideas for finding new revenue, many directors don't understand enough about IT to keep up. In many boardrooms, discussions about IT issues can be measured in minutes.

In a *CIO* survey of 250 IT leaders, 64 percent said the board "doesn't do its homework" about technology matters and 57 percent said directors rely heavily on what they read in the press to evaluate IT strategy. Some 40 percent say board members "don't really care about IT." The Board Institute, which educates and evaluates directors about corporate governance, says that only six percent of companies have a board-level technology committee, where directors focus on the strategic use of IT.

Innovation Advisory Board

A relatively new use of advisory boards is to address product design and innovation. In fact, some of the products lining supermarket shelves or displayed in the windows of a favorite store may have been created, packaged, marketed, or improved with the help of a design or innovation advisory board. Such a board lets a company tap into outside thinking from a multitude of sources, thereby getting an opportunity to hear from the best and the brightest, to invite new thinking among its own people, and even to transform its culture.

Margaret Pederson, President of Amirexx, a director of Viad, Xamax Industries, and TextureMedia, Inc., and an advisory board member of WCD, says innovation is a board responsibility: "Innovation is not limited to any industry sector, geographic region, or timeframe. Forward-thinking companies are using innovation advisory boards or committees to help identify and address changes in the marketplace and competitive landscape. Working with management, these groups identify new products, services, processes, and technologies that maintain or improve the company's position and secure new leadership opportunities. In the Price Waterhouse Coopers study of 1,757 C-suite executives *Breakthrough Innovation and Growth*, 43 percent called innovation a competitive necessity and 93 said that organic growth through innovation would drive the greater proportion of their revenue growth."

Environmental Advisory Board

An article in the *Wall Street Journal*, "More Companies Bow to Investors With a Social Cause," lays out the importance of being alert to "soft" matters: "Shareholders are driving changes in corporate policies and disclosures unthinkable a decade ago, on issues ranging from protecting rain forests to human rights ... So far this year, environmental and social issues have accounted for 56 percent of shareholder proposals, representing a majority for the first time ... That is up from about 40 percent in the previous two years, and means shareholders are increasingly voting on things like greenhouse-gas emissions, political spending, and labor rights."

As various groups (the public, churches, trade unions, consumers, non-governmental organizations, and government agencies) press for social responsibility, CEOs are coming to understand that the demand for "sustainable" products and services will only increase. Since the complexity of global issues requires more than the inspired vision of a single individual, companies are using environmental advisory boards to gain valuable insights into new solutions, new markets, and new ways of doing business. The good news: An ethical stance can provide a bottom-line boost, especially with the rise of the green consumer.

Risk Advisory Board

In a survey of corporate board members, Spencer Stuart asked directors "What would improve your board's ability to oversee risk?" Thirty-three percent said "a separate risk committee."

Of course, risk takes many different forms, and the role of a risk advisory board would vary depending on the company's industry and scope of business. A manufacturer might have risks in its supply chain if its facilities or suppliers are located in potentially volatile regions of the world. Contingency plans — for everything from political unrest to natural disaster — can be reviewed by a risk advisory board with a global perspective. The board of a financial services company might set up a risk advisory board to keep track of evolving and emerging regulations around the world. A health care enterprise might need risk oversight for everything from pharmaceuticals to patient rights.

The risk advisory board brings together people with expertise in governance, risk management, and compliance. Their insights can help the board contribute to effective strategy and operations, on a regional, national, and global scale.

COMPARE AND CONTRAST

Board Of Directors	Advisory Board
Provides governance and binding advice	Provides guidance and non-binding advice
Terms are not very flexible: expect three year terms, and expect to be re-elected two or three times for a total of nine to twelve years	Flexible in term length (we recommend a one-year term which gives leverage to change as needed)
Fiduciary and legal responsibilities	No fiduciary or legal responsibilities
Regulated by Sarbanes-Oxley (SOX)	Flexible in mandate: can be created to address specific organizational needs and disbanded as soon as goals are met
Majority independent	Candid, forthright advisors
Committees – Audit – Compensation – Nomination – Governance and others	Skills and experience more important than rank; experts companies can't afford to hire
Board self assessment	Assessed by board and management
Large commitment of time	Less commitment of time
Flexible in compensation; higher fees to directors	Less in fees, creative compensation or stock
D&O insurance	No D&O insurance

Source: OnBoard BootCamp

A SPECIAL CASE: THE FAMILY BUSINESS BOARD

"The greatest ability in business is to get along with others and to influence their actions."

– John Hancock

Family-controlled businesses represent nearly 35 percent of Fortune 500 companies. What's more, "family-run companies generate 78 percent of new jobs in the U.S.," says Anne Berner, CEO of Vallila Interior, a director of Koskisen Oy, Kährs PLC and European Family Businesses in Brussels, co-chair of WCD Family Business Council and co-chair of WCD Finland Chapter. "But the even greater role they play around the world – from Asia to Europe – underlines the value of understanding and improving their governance practices."

WCD launched the Family Business Council in June 2014 which is slated to conduct a number of initiatives, including: new programs for women CEOs and directors of family companies around both the WCD Global Institute as well as its regional institutes, research with Spencer Stuart, Professor Boris Groysberg, PhD, of the Harvard Business School and organizational behavior expert and researcher Deborah Bell, to identify specific skills needed for the family/private-owned company board service as well as the particular challenges faced by these businesses today; and director introductions, both for family businesses seeking outside directors and for family business leaders looking to broaden their experience through public-company board service. In addition, the 2015 WCD Thought Leadership Council, chaired by KPMG, will tackle the topic of global corporate governance of family businesses.

If you're invited to serve on a private-company board, you should know that extra traits come in handy. For example, Stephanie Sonnabend, Co-founder and Chair of 2020 Women on Boards, former CEO and President of Sonesta International Hotels Corporation and a director of Century Bank, Century Bancorp, and Sperry Van Ness, cautions that it's important to be sensitive to the needs and issues of the founder/family and how these interface with the business:

"While board members represent outside shareholders, they must represent the family interests as well. The board's role is to encourage the leader to manage both and not ignore difficult issues, such as competing interests and succession planning. It is often difficult to impose strict governance procedures, so it is best to move slowly. While board meetings may be considered a good training ground for future family leaders, it is best to leave family involvement to a minimum and allow family members to participate in annual meetings or a family council."

Elaine J. Eisenman, PhD, Dean and Professor of Management practice of Babson Executive Education and a director of DSW and Harvard Vanguard Medical Associates, co-chair of WCD Boston Chapter and an advisory board member of WCD, cautions that, while the governance responsibilities of boards of private and public companies are the same, the differences between the two types can be significant: "When a company's CEO is also the majority shareholder, the board's contribution is 'advice and counsel' rather than 'advice and approval.' Sitting on such boards is not for the faint of heart or for those who are unwilling to speak truth to power."

She sets these expectations for anyone serving on the board of a family business:

- You should make sure that the CEO has the experience, strategic direction, and vision necessary to grow the company. Your role is to protect the shareholder, who is also the CEO, which includes telling the CEO when he is acting in his personal, short-term interests rather than the company's best, long-term interests. This can also mean insuring that the compensation and discretionary spending of the CEO (and family members) doesn't harm the company's financial health.
- You should help the founder/CEO see when it is time to start grooming a successor and, ultimately, when it's time to step down. In this decision (and all others related to management hiring and development), you'll likely need to help the CEO make decisions based on objective measures rather than gut feeling. It's important that the company move beyond the original leadership team and bring in professional managers who have critical and strategic skill sets. (Be forewarned: the CEO's personal loyalties and the needs of the company can clash).
- Also, the board will have to be sure that its skills match the company's needs based on its stage of growth, not just immediate, but also in the future. Board

meetings should have agendas with a strategic focus; they should not be opportunities for the CEO to play show-and-tell.

- You need to be comfortable having your ideas, recommendations, and warnings debated and/or ignored. If disagreements are continual, and if the CEO stops listening to your knowledge-based advice, it will probably be necessary to step down.

How close are family boards getting to this ideal?

In the WCD/Heidrick & Struggles *2013 Board of Directors Survey*, directors on family boards ranked their performance as "less effective" on almost every measure. For example, the majority said their succession practices are inadequate (see the sidebar, "A sticky subject: Succession planning in a family business" on page 174).

The majority also said that their board misses some vital skills, especially HR-Talent management (a deficit that goes hand-in-hand with poor succession planning). Also, less than one-quarter said they had a process of determining what combination of skills and attributes is required for the board. A low percentage said they are advancing diversity on their boards and in their companies.

Richard M. Clarke, Co-founder and a Managing Partner of The CEO Perspective Group, suggests these ten tips for being an excellent director on the board of a family-run business:

1. Learn and remember the beliefs, principles and driving forces of the founder(s). They may still have substantial significance to how the company is run today.

2. Growth in economic value is important; however, it is not the sole measurement of success. This is especially true if a profit focus damages the ability for continuation of generational ownership.

3. Maintain as clear an understanding of the shareholders' overall desires as possible. In a family business they are owners, as opposed to simply investors. Blood is thicker than earnings per share!

4. Understand the key non-financial values that the family owners hold dear. This will provide additional insight as to how you can be a successful member of the board-management leadership team.

5. All families have differences of opinions, and as the family groups grow in number, the differences grow in both quantity and complexity. You can't solve them all, but it behooves you to recognize the current major ones that could impinge on how the business is run.

6. The "patience quotient" in a family-owned company is usually of a much longer time frame than what exists in a publicly-traded company. Evaluate what the PQ factor is in your company and determine the best way to work within that.

7. Make sure that a top-ranked goal for the board is to have succession plans in place for the chairperson and the CEO (two people, not one). Equally important, is to check from time to time the family agreement with these overall plans, including a thorough determination of the merits of a family member candidate.

8. If a family advisory council doesn't exist, form one! If one does exist, don't ignore it! Learn how to include this council in company affairs/issues. This is not to be interpreted to mean the council has direct impact on running the company.

9. Spend sufficient time assessing the "risk tolerance" of the family owners. This is particularly true for those owners who have been instrumental in building the company to its current level. Knowledge of the risk/reward ratio is critical for establishing acceptable growth strategies.

10. Get to know the wants and desires of the younger generation. The men and women who are now in high school or college will soon be influencing the future of the company, and one of them just might be your next chairperson or CEO.

Consider Using an Advisory Board

Advisory boards can be an excellent tool for family businesses. For example, one family enterprise, EHR Investments Inc., created an advisory board for its aviation financing business —EHR Aviation Inc. — to help determine the best approach for dispensing with repossessed aircraft. EHR Investments' President and CEO, Susan Remmer Ryzewic, notes that the advisory board members had deep knowledge of the market and its key players. An added benefit for Ryzewic was the personal relationship she was able to form with the advisory board members and how helpful their expertise has continued to be, even after the completion of the board's term. "Needless to say, I wish that I had established the advisory board earlier," says Remmer Ryzewic, who is also a director of Endless Pools, Inc., and William Smith Enterprises, Inc. and co-chair of WCD Family Business Council and WCD North Florida and South Georgia Chapter. "We might have avoided some of our business pitfalls."

A STICKY SUBJECT: SUCCESSION PLANNING IN A FAMILY BUSINESS

While planning for the succession of top leaders is critically important, in a family business it's often neglected. Spencer Stuart offers this perspective:

"Family companies, which are typically closely aligned with the founder and sometimes with a family member serving as CEO, generally lack a planned succession. There are either too few or too many potential candidates, which creates confusion and uncertainty for investors, customers, suppliers and employees. But family businesses that are not prepared for an orderly management turnover may be setting the scene for a disruptive battle in the boardroom and, perhaps, the courtroom.

"How can family companies ensure that they have the right leadership on hand when they need it? First, by positioning themselves for the future by investing in robust leadership development and succession planning processes, adapting succession planning best practices to the unique characteristics of family-owned businesses. Second, by understanding the competitive landscape for talent, the different characteristics of family, private equity and public companies, and the motivations of executives best suited to a family company role. Third, by knowing when it may be necessary or appropriate to consider candidates from outside the organization and what to look for in those candidates.

"The board can help by providing an objective process for succession planning that includes developing criteria for future leadership, benchmarking internal candidates, and identifying skill gaps."

My First Board — JUDI NORTH

"I joined my first board — Winn-Dixie — in the early '90s, when I was the head of Bell South's consumer business. While Winn-Dixie was a public company, it still had a very strong family influence. When the last founding brother died, the new CEO realized that 'no female representation' had been a rule.

"The CEO said to the chairman of Bell South, 'I don't even know any business woman to promote because we don't have any women executives.' The chairman replied that he'd introduce the CEO to four or five women, but first he could 'practice' on me. The three of us met for lunch and started talking. Because there was no pressure, the conversation was easy. At the end, the CEO asked me to join the board. Later, the chairman said to me, 'I was going to tell you what you needed to change to become a serious candidate for a board, but apparently you did okay.'

"For quite some time, I was the only woman on the Winn-Dixie board. But, like most women executives, I knew how to be the minority. The first step is figuring out the board's culture. Are people thoughtful when they speak? Do they encourage give-and-take? Then, you do what you do best."

A CASE STUDY IN FRUSTRATION AND FAILURE

Background

Company Y is a third-generation family business in the consumer goods industry. It was founded in Europe before WWII and relocated to the United States by the second generation in the early 1950s. Two sons of the founder serve as co-CEOs; each has two children who work in sales in the company.

When the CEOs realized that the company was stuck in "maintenance mode" with minimal growth opportunities, they formed an advisory board of outsiders to address the problem.

The Challenge

The underlying dynamic of this family business was conflict and competition.

Each sibling believed that his ideas were smarter, more clever and creative, and best for the company – not surprising since when they were growing up they were told that they were equal in power and skill (and always would be). That myth was destructive in two ways: 1) it failed to recognize the different competencies of each brother, and 2) it rendered impossible efficient and effective decision making. The only power each CEO had was to block and/or sabotage the other. The company's lack of growth was a natural outcome of this paralysis, and the unspoken agenda for the advisory board was to fix the problem.

Lessons Learned

Each member of the advisory board had significant experience in founder-led and/or family-owned businesses. Each accepted the role with an understanding that the CEOs had agreed to create an aggressive growth plan for the company, and that part of this plan was to create a logical succession plan based on the changing needs of the company.

The dysfunction of the company's management structure was not immediately apparent, and for the first year the CEOs engaged with the board in evaluating the company's positioning in an increasingly competitive marketplace. Organic and potential acquisition targets were identified, the financials were reviewed and addressed, the children were interviewed, and opportunities were identified.

Slowly, the board members began to realize that no real action was being taken.

Escalating grievances between the brothers and obfuscating actions by the next generations ensured on-going stagnation. The advisory board worked hard to address the underlying dynamics, but to no avail. The brothers showed increasing levels of denial and resistance to any discussions that went beyond the airing of grievances. As the board members tried collectively and individually to intervene with each brother, the CEOs insisted on bringing in an experienced CEO from outside, while they would take on advisory roles. A search firm was engaged, a job description written, and a search begun; then, the expected explosion occurred. The brothers rejected every candidate, while blaming each other for being overly emotional and controlling. After much soul searching, the advisory board resigned.

The key lesson learned: assess the readiness of the family to listen to outsiders before joining a board.

Source: Elaine J. Eisenman, PhD

THE ABCS OF FRAUD AND MISCONDUCT

"I am afraid we must make the world honest before we can honestly say to our children that honesty is the best policy."

– George Bernard Shaw

One concern that's taken center stage in corporate boardrooms (because of the growing complexity of the regulatory environment in the US and abroad) is the risk of fraud and misconduct. If a company acts inappropriately, the fallout can include significant harm to its reputation, the economic costs of investigations, fines, and penalties, and the criminal prosecution of individuals.

Here's a summary of some relevant regulations:
- Dodd-Frank Whistleblower provisions (2010) offer incentives to those reporting misconduct, specifically 10-30 percent of funds seized in excess of $1 million USD. Whistleblowers are not required to report internally first.
- The US Foreign Corrupt Practices Act (1977) prohibits illicit payments by US companies to foreign officials; its enforcement is a top priority for the SEC, Department of Justice, and foreign regulators; 33 US trading partners have enacted similar regulations.
- The UK Bribery Act (2010) extends anti-corruption law to further reduce bribery in UK to include commercial party bribery (active and passive offenses), persons acting on behalf of a commercial organization, and people and entities not registered in the UK. The act requires companies to show efforts to prevent bribery.
- The Russia Anti-Corruption Law (2011) criminalizes the bribery of public officials.
- China Anti-Corruption Laws(2012) have made the receipt of gifts of substantial value from foreign interests illegal.
- India Anti-Corruption Laws(2011) punish public officers who collect bribes with six months to five years in prison.

As a director, you should ask pointed questions of your company's leadership:

- How effective is the company's compliance program in managing risks related to cross-border or other fraud and misconduct compliance requirements? Do compliance efforts cross functions and divisions? Does the company have a chief compliance or risk officer? And does he/she report to the audit committee, at least annually, on the status quo, while advising promptly on matters involving criminal misconduct?

- Are the compliance programs enabled by technology?

- To comply with regulations, has the company put in place policies, procedures, internal controls; training and communications; and diligence processes for the evaluation of third-party agents, vendors, and contractors?

- Are compliance plans aligned with strategic objectives, such as mergers and acquisitions, global expansion plans, and sourcing decisions? How effective is management's strategic planning process in dealing with the pace of innovation and technology change on the business?

"The board of any US company with operations in China needs to have a clear understanding of its duties and responsibilities under the Foreign Corrupt Practices Act (FCPA) and other international laws... Investigations and prosecutions have risen dramatically in recent years, resulting in 12 discrete FCPA actions in 2012 alone, six of which were healthcare-related, leading to $260 million in fines. In fact, 20 percent of FCPA enforcement actions in the past five years have involved business conduct in China. The reputational and economic ramifications of misinterpreting these duties and responsibilities can have a long-lasting impact on the economics and reputation of the company. China's emergence as a significant market means that governance issues are more important than ever in board and management's risk considerations. China has its own version of anti-bribery laws, as well, which in many instances is stricter and more severe than international laws. Effectively addressing governance structures and issues in China is increasingly leading to best practices for all international markets."

Eric V. Zwisler | President of Cardinal Health China and past CEO of Zuellig Pharma Asia Pacific in his NACD Directorship article "Corruption in China and Elsewhere Demands Board Oversight."

QUESTIONS EVERY DIRECTOR SHOULD ASK ABOUT LIABILITY

"All power is a trust ... we are accountable for its exercise."
— Benjamin Disraeli

One of the unfortunate realities of board service is the risk of lawsuits filed against directors, says LouAnn Layton, Managing Director of Marsh & McLennan Companies and a director of FIVER. "While most boards and the directors act with the utmost of care, complying with all laws and regulations, they're still not immune to litigation because shareholders and other stakeholders can sue a company when they believe that decisions made put the business and its financials in jeopardy."

Layton contributed the following discussion about questions every director should ask about liability.

What are a director's legal obligations?

"The fundamental fiduciary duties of corporate directors under state law are the duty of loyalty and the duty of care. The duty of care generally requires that directors act prudently and in a reasonably informed manner in their oversight of corporate affairs. A director may violate the duty of care by making a decision negligently or failing to act in circumstances in which a director paying due attention to corporate affairs would have acted.

"The duty of loyalty generally requires that directors act in good faith and in the best interests of the corporation and its shareholders. It entails avoiding conflicts of interest, the usurpation of corporate opportunities and self-dealing. In short, the duty of loyalty mandates that the interests of the corporation and its shareholders take precedence over the interests of the director. The duty to act in good faith may sometimes be characterized as distinct from the duty of loyalty.

"Flowing from the fundamental duties of loyalty and care is what is sometimes referred to as the duty of candor or disclosure, which mandates that disclosures to shareholders be complete and accurate.

In addition, corporate directors are subject to specific statutory requirements."

What are a director's sources of liability?

"Directors have many sources of potential liability. First and foremost is the potential liability to the corporation or its shareholders for breach of fiduciary duty or, in the case of public held corporations, violations of the securities laws. In recent years, claims for breach of fiduciary duties follow almost invariably in the M&A context when boards seek shareholder approval for the transaction. More generally, any corporate debacle may give rise to derivative litigation alleging mismanagement.

"Sources of potential liability are by no means limited to exposure to shareholder related claims. They encompass third parties as well. Directors of insolvent or nearly insolvent corporations may owe fiduciary duties to creditors, who are seen to stand in the shoes of the shareholders. Directors may also be subject to claims by employees for violation of federal or state statutes or state common law governing the employer-employee relationship. Although some statutes limit liability to the 'employer,' not all do, notably the Fair Labor Standards Act. Directors may also face liability under ERISA as fiduciaries of corporate welfare and benefit plans.

"Directors also face exposure to claims by third parties. For example, competitors may assert anti-trust or intellectual property related claims, as well as common law tort, not only against the corporation itself, but against the directors. Civil and criminal claims by government agencies are another source of potential exposure to directors. Environmental laws, securities laws, tax laws and, at least for directors of certain corporations, the Foreign Corrupt Practices Act are examples of such exposures."

What indemnification obligations should a director expect to receive from the company?

"There are three main vehicles of indemnification for directors: the certificate of incorporation, corporate bylaws, and indemnification agreements between the corporation and individual board members. Overlaying this structure is the D&O insurance a company may carry, which can help to reimburse the costs incurred by the company in indemnifying the directors. In certain cases, D&O insurance also serves as a fourth source of recovery for the director, when the company either cannot (i.e., for reasons of insolvency), or will not (i.e., due to concerns about the individual's conduct) indemnify the director.

"It is worth noting that D&O insurance does not cover every type of claim. Even when coverage is ultimately triggered, there are often legal fees incurred in the early stages of an investigation which are considered outside the scope of covered loss, so the question arises as to how these costs are to be borne. There is an important distinction between 'indemnification' and 'advancement.' While a director would not see any recovery through indemnification until the conclusion of the legal proceeding, advancement obligates the company to pay legal fees as the costs are incurred. Which of these is required should be spelled out in the Certificate of Incorporation and/or the bylaws; if the two are in conflict, the director can assert that the more favorable one should govern.

"Increasingly, public companies are using indemnification agreements to supplement the protection already afforded directors through other corporate instruments. Indemnification agreements can provide for even more specific terms of indemnification, such as the process and time frames for reimbursement, avenues of appeal in the event the company denies a director's request, and approval of indemnification for outside directorship activity."

Can a company refuse to indemnify?

"Generally, a company's ability (and sometimes its obligation) to indemnify is governed by rules appearing in the corporate governance statutes of a particular jurisdiction. These jurisdictions — state, province, or country — often differ in their approach or views. As such, a company's ability to make choices about indemnification depends on what the law of their incorporation allows. Under most corporate governance codes, a company may refuse to indemnify."

What does a properly constructed D&O contract look like?

"A properly constructed D&O policy will contain three insuring clauses: Clause A coverage protecting individual directors and officers for non-indemnifiable loss, Clause B coverage (aka corporate reimbursement insurance) reimbursing the corporation for its indemnification of a director or officer for the director or officers liability for loss, and Clause C coverage (aka entity coverage) usually limited to protecting the corporation for liability for securities claims. Every D&O policy should have broad-based definitions of "Loss and Claim" and contain no more than six exclusions. A D&O policy must also contain severability provisions for exclusions, duties of cooperation and application representation, as well as appropriate priority of payments provisions. The policy should eliminate or limit presumptive indemnification and allocation clauses."

How does one know that limits are adequate?

"The choice for limits purchasing is ultimately made by the buyer. However, with effective guidance and counsel from expert insurance broker advisors, the buyer has the ability to purchase limits that will provide the necessary protection to mitigate the financial impact of a D&O loss to directors and officers and their corporations. The use of industry peer benchmarking data and risk modeling effectively eliminates guesswork and fosters an ability to make an informed judgment on the proper limits."

What are the five most important contract provisions?

"While D&O contracts can vary from carrier to carrier, most contain the same basic provisions. Directors should review the applicable policy form with a view toward understanding these provisions:

"'Claim' defines which actions and proceedings will trigger coverage. This definition should be as broad as possible. Typically, a policy provides coverage for written demands for monetary, non-monetary or injunctive relief, as well as for civil, criminal, administrative, and regulatory proceedings. It should also include coverage for a director who becomes the target of a civil, criminal, or regulatory investigation. Some policies also cover 'pre-claim' matters such as when a director is asked by a regulator to appear for a meeting or interview or to produce documents to the regulator in connection with the director or officer's role with the organization.

"'Loss' defines what will be covered if a claim results in liability for a director. This definition should be as broad as possible. Covered items of loss typically include damages, settlements, judgments (including pre/post judgment interest), and defense costs. Uncovered items may include certain fines and penalties, taxes, and matters uninsurable as a matter of law.

"D&O policies typically contain exclusions for certain personal conduct on the part of insured, including claims involving criminal and/or fraudulent acts and claims involving improper personal profit or advantage. 'Personal conduct' exclusions require some form of proof before the exclusion is triggered.

"Severability provisions in D&O policies address the extent to which the insurer may void or rescind coverage based on material misrepresentations or non-disclosures in the application process. The policy should contain language providing that the application for coverage will be treated as a separate application for each director and that the knowledge of one director will not be imputed to another for the purpose of determining coverage.

"Most policies will have a mechanism in place to pay loss within the applicable retention in the event the organization can indemnify for such loss but fails or refuses to do so. With respect to non-indemnifiable loss, most policies also provide for advancement of covered defense costs or pre-claim costs, often no later than 90 days after the insurer's receipt of bills evidencing such costs."

If I am sued as a director, what should I expect?

"If you find yourself the target of a lawsuit, expect to receive a high-quality defense from an experienced attorney at the expense of the company you serve. Indeed, even where the lawsuit alleges intentional fraud, criminal act, or other intentional wrongdoing, a director should expect to have his or her legal defenses funded until such time as a final, non-appealable court judgment of liability/guilt is rendered.

"Take these steps promptly upon receiving notice of the lawsuit and during the litigation process:

"Provide a copy of the operative complaint (or demand letter or other warning of potential suit, if a complaint has not yet been filed) to the company's general counsel and request confirmation that the lawsuit has been noticed to the D&O insurer. It is important that notice be sent to the D&O insurer as soon as possible after receipt of the complaint (or earlier document), as failure to promptly notice a claim can potentially compromise coverage under the D&O policy.

"Be sure the D&O insurer approves the chosen defense attorney and agrees to pay his or her rates (certain D&O policies will require that a director choose counsel from a pre-established list). In most policies, the insurer is responsible only for costs to which it has consented.

"Once defense counsel is approved and hired, make sure that the attorneys

① D&O offered by Chub

② Large corporations offer D&O for employees

understand and comply with their obligation to provide the insurer with periodic status updates and copies of their invoices. Failure to do so can delay payment and, in extreme cases, compromise coverage.

"Ensure that defense counsel understands that he or she may not enter into settlement discussions without first obtaining consent from the insurer. Failure to do so can be grounds for the insurer to deny coverage for any settlement amounts later paid.

"Expect to provide a lot of documents (paper and electronic) to defense counsel concerning the decisions or transactions at issue in the lawsuit. The lawsuit will likely be settled before trial, usually funded entirely by the company and/or its D&O insurers. But if the suit is not settled, expect to testify at deposition and trial. Any failure to cooperate with these obligations can prejudice the defense, create more liability, and compromise insurance coverage.

"While litigation is almost always unpleasant for a defendant, and particularly for a director where the nature of the allegations (breach of fiduciary duty, securities fraud, etc.) are often personally offensive, these steps above can at least ensure that a director's legal costs will be paid promptly and in full by the company."

WHAT'S IN A NAME? EVERYTHING

"It takes 20 years to build a reputation and five minutes to ruin it. If you think about that, you'll do things differently."

– Warren Buffet

Consider these facts. More than five billion people are texting, tweeting and browsing on mobile phones worldwide. Thirty billion pieces of content are shared on Facebook every month. People upload 48 hours of new video to YouTube every minute of every day, according to Wikibon Blog. That's a lot of potential exposure — good or bad — for companies and individuals.

The importance of image management is argued in the *Agenda* article, "Boards Coming Up Short on Crisis Management," written by Marcy Syms, Partner and President of TPD Group LLC, and a director of Rite Aid, and Davia Temin, President and CEO of Temin and Company, Inc., and an advisory board member of WCD.

Companies working in a media-saturated, global economy cannot hide a miss-step. At the same time, they potentially face crises of a "magnitude never before seen … ranging from workplace safety disasters and massive trading losses, to data breaches and financial mismanagement,"

The two conclude that the way corporate boards respond to a crisis reveals much about the character and culture of the organizations they lead. Board members should have plans in place for crisis management, beginning with the formation of a "crisis committee" and the identification of the director who could act decisively in a crisis. Syms and Temin also suggest a "crisis boot camp" to help directors prepare to respond effectively in various scenarios. Of course, every board should be thoroughly familiar with its company's crisis plan.

"No matter how you define it, corporate reputation has become one of the biggest, albeit intangible, assets or liabilities a company has, and thus an important consideration for the board of directors."

Davia Temin | President and CEO of Temin and Company, Inc., and an advisory board member of WCD, in *Directors & Boards*

My First Board — **PAT MCKAY**

"It came up, as these things sometimes do, unexpectedly — in my case, from people I'd known over the years. I had just become the CFO of a publicly-traded company when I got asked to join a board. But the company was on the other side of the country, so I thought to myself, 'Good grief, how am I possibly going to be able to accomplish that?' I turned the offer down.

"Then a friend — actually, a member of WomenCorporateDirectors — said, 'Pat, you absolutely have to meet with the chairman of this board and talk about the opportunity,' and so I did. Subsequently, I met with other members of the board and, one thing leading to another, and I joined.

"My first board was very progressive — there were three other women board members. Because it was a retail-oriented company, the board represented a really good match between the opportunities for women on boards and the company's strategic mission. We could do an excellent job of thinking about which and how goods should be delivered to customers."

"Every great dream begins with a dreamer. Always remember, you have **within you** the **strength,** the **patience,** and the **passion** to reach for the stars.**"**

– Harriet Tubman

Margaret Mead understood the power of working together: "Never doubt that a small group of thoughtful, committed citizens can change the world; indeed, it's the only thing that ever has." As a director, you can help an enterprise leave a positive mark on everyone it touches, everywhere in the wide world. This section offers advice, both pragmatic and aspirational, on doing your job as a director.

"Women are the disruptive innovation of the next century. We are the ones who bring up issues that others may not be thinking of. For example, when infrastructure is lacking and people don't get electricity and water, that's not just a technical problem. It's the woman leader who inevitably says, 'This is a question of dignity' and that's the kind of thinking companies need to move into the next century."

Usha Rao-Monari
a director and CEO of Global Water Development Partners,
a Blackstone Portfolio Company

SUCCEEDING AS A DIRECTOR AND CREATING VISIONARY BOARDS

KNOW, THEN ACT: THAT'S THE SECRET TO POSITIVE CHANGE

"If we could first know where we are, and whither we are tending, we could then better judge what to do, and how to do it."
— Abraham Lincoln

You can't change behavior or outcomes without first taking stock. Enrico Fermi summed up the value of assessing what's what: "There are two possible outcomes: if the result confirms the hypothesis, then you've made a measurement. If the result is contrary to the hypothesis, then you've made a discovery."

Great directors go to the edge of business issues, openly bringing up the unanswered questions, and encouraging discussion. If at least 40 percent of the total board time is not a general and engaged discussion, as opposed to directors listening to presentations, you are at serious risk of getting far less value. Visionary boards spend time on forward looking issues, not just backward looking ones.

Board members, as individuals and as a group, need to define their "as is" position, assess their performance, and decide on a "to be" goal. No improvement can be made without a long and honest look in the mirror. For OnBoard Bootcamp, KPMG developed this list of self-assessment questions as a first step toward becoming an optimally effective board. As you answer these questions, look for improvement opportunities.

- What is the board's governance model? Has it changed over time? Is it still optimal given new or emerging conditions (in the company, in the industry, and in the global marketplace)? Are you, as a group, envisioning a "future board" whose members would have the expertise and experience to address the changing external environment and evolving strategic priorities?

- What is the board's role in developing and critiquing strategy? How much leeway exists to question or challenge proposals? What is the best way to delineate responsibility for developing, discussing, fine tuning and executing strategy? What is the right balance between advice and control?

- How is the board adding value to the company? Is each director's skills and experience still relevant to the company's success? Does the board have the right mix of expertise and is this expertise being used productively? Where is the board, as a group, falling short?

- Is the prevailing board atmosphere collegial or tense? How do you resolve conflicts or address disruptive behavior? Who's making sure the each member is able to contribute his or her best thinking? Are you striking the right balance in how you spend your time during meetings?

- What is the right balance between broad-based business experience and specialist expertise on a board? Is your annual assessment process rigorous and thorough?

- Is your succession planning methodology (for the CEO, the executive committee, the chairman, and new board directors) rigorous and value-driven? Does the board have contingencies for both planned and emergency successions? Do you have a clear line of sight into the executive ranks below the executive committee? Does the board have the tools to assess potential successors?

- How does the board assess and supervise risk? Does this approach take into account new and emerging risks (such as cyber security)? How does the board work with the C-suite in managing risk? What is the company's and the board's appetite for risk? Is it too great or too small, given the company's competitive positioning? To what extent do personal considerations affect each director's attitude to risk? Can the board identify the organization's risks? Does the board spend time on "what if" thinking? Is a heightened awareness of risk stifling innovation and creativity in the executive team? Does the board stay alert to reputational risk?

- Does the board have enough information to make wise decisions? Are decisions being made in the long-term interests of the enterprise? For example, is the idea of "corporate responsibility" defined and discussed? Does the company's strategy address its role in global sustainability and climate change? How do board members stay current? Does the board provide continual education? Are you happy with the quality of board-level communication, both internally and externally?

- How does the board assess its own performance? Liane Pelletier, a director of Expeditors International and Atlantic Tele Network, lead director of Washington Federal, and Chair of Icicle Seafoods, says her board has had great success with written, anonymous evaluation surveys asking the board members to assess important matters: setting board agendas, engaging in corporate strategy development, and defining how best to review regularly both emergency and planned executive succession. Once the survey is complete and the responses summarized, the full board can use the insights gained to decide on an action plan for improvement. "The anonymity, and the explicit expectation that board members write comments alongside each numerically scored question, resulted in information and inputs that don't naturally surface when we are together, even in executive session," says Pelletier.

"It's very important to have a robust performance management system, including a very clear personal development plan for executives in the organization. We call ours 3 + 1 — three goals for the business, one goal for personal development. In this way, we've created a strong performance culture which focuses everyone on results. That benefits the business and promotes diversity."

Paul Polman | CEO of Unilever, and winner of the WCD Visionary Award for Leadership and Governance of a Public Company in his address at the third annual WCD Global Institute

ACTION TIPS

To be a great board member:

Be the most well prepared director in the room. Study the board book and ask questions in advance.

Be a student of the company and the industry. Join industry trade groups, subscribe to industry magazines, follow the company and industry on Twitter, and sign up to receive press releases about the company and their competitors.

Visit different locations and meet with different employee groups. Be sure to meet with young women on all your visits. You'll be a great role model and you'll end up understanding the company better (particularly in foreign countries).

WE TALK TO A DIVERSITY CHAMPION: SIR GERRY GRIMSTONE

Sir Gerry Grimstone, Chairman of Standard Life plc and TheCityUK, lead non-executive director of the Ministry of Defence and an independent director of Deloitte LLP, addressed the WomenCorporateDirectors European Institute and answered members' questions.

> **When you're constructing a board, what's your thought process?**

"I'm very organized. Across the top of a chart I list the qualities I want in a board member. These could be anything — customer-facing experience, technology experience, regulatory experience — I end up with 15 or 20. Down the side I list 25 or 30 candidates. I mark each one 'red,' 'amber' or 'green' for each quality. I analyze skill sets very, very deliberately — it's a question of getting the right kind of orchestra of talent.

"I think I have a real responsibility to develop my board members. So, I don't just leave them alone. A great board day for me is one in which every director is involved; I feel very disappointed if everyone doesn't speak on every topic. I want us all to go home in the evening thinking that the company is in a better position at the end of the day than it was at the beginning."

> **What can a woman bring to a board that's different from what a man brings?**

"I don't like really thinking about it in terms of men and women. I just want an intellectually diverse mix. Putting together a board is like making a curry: it's the mix of the spices that matters. You don't want one spice to overpower the pot: you want harmony. I think women can play in creating coherence.

"I abhor factions on boards. I hate it when people aren't happy to speak out openly and transparently. I'm really disappointed if people are huddling in corners or meeting in little groups, muttering to each other. That would be a failure on my part, because that kind of behavior is divisive and corrosive."

> **You sit on boards in China, India, and the UK. How do they compare? What are the differences?**

"There are far fewer differences than you might imagine. In China and India, people are sensitive about their positions in the world. That said, I think the Chinese are completely gender-blind at the board level. Also, there are very powerful women on Indian boards. In India, the challenge is getting people to speak up. But as an outsider, I can cut through the hierarchy."

> **In your experience, what percentage of the typical board agenda is forward-looking?**

"In a regulated entity, I'd say probably 30-40 percent of our time is spent on things we have to do, which are driven by the reporting cycle. So there's no choice about that. But what's surprised me is that the rest of the time — 50-60 percent — is open. It's very important that the chairman takes control of that time. So, I use an elaborate rolling process which allows me to think about the agenda three months out and six months out. I plan those agendas, and then refine them as the meetings get closer. That allows me to put together agendas that cut across many, different business units.

"I should mention, we run a very, very strong self-appraisal system. We keep a record of what every non-executive does in the business, and we encourage their deep involvement. The greater their knowledge, the better our work in strategy and everything else."

THE POWER OF PLANNING: SETTING THE AGENDA

"Our goals can only be reached through a vehicle of a plan, in which we must fervently believe, and upon which we must vigorously act. There is no other route to success."

– Pablo Picasso

The old saying "plan the work, then work the plan" is a good rule to live by for board meetings. Having a good agenda helps ensure that a few necessary things happen during the meeting itself.

Strategic issues will rise to the surface, thereby helping assure that the meeting itself is used for productive discussion. A focused, well-considered agenda frees the board to address the issues that matter — the ones that center on keeping the organization safe, solvent, and compliant with global and local regulations. "The agenda is like the screen for an air traffic controller: If you don't watch carefully, the right issues won't come up. You have to actively control what comes to the board meeting," says Suzy Walton, PhD, board deputy chairman of Manufactures and Commerce (RSA), a director of the Institute of Directors, a director and Chairman of Medical Services Committee, Combat Stress, and member of State Honours Committee.

Board members can be better prepared. Melanie Barstad, retired President of Acute Care of Johnson & Johnson and a director of CINTAS and Auburn University Foundation, says that the agenda allows her to look for one or two key points or questions on each topic, so that her contributions are value-added and her thoughts carefully considered and succinct. "Well articulated, factually stated recommendations are received with respect," she says.

Some topics can be set a year in advance (for example, a budget review in February and a year-end review in November). Other topics, such as SEC regulations or good governance, are covered at every meeting. The more dynamic issues that should make it on an agenda can include emerging strategies, risk management (including cyber security), social media, sustainability, and data management.

Board books should be sent at least one week in advance. Hot topics should be listed so directors can have the time to think about them before the meeting. In *Boardroom INSIDER*, this "fresh idea" is offered for setting an agenda: "Leave a blank space on the preliminary agenda; when you circulate it to board members, ask for items they want to cover." The advantage of this approach is that more directors will get involved in setting the agenda and more will, therefore, be engaged in the work of the meeting.

What are some best practices for agenda-setting, according to WomenCorporateDirectors members?

Michelle Goldberg, a Partner at Ignition, and a director at Moz, Glympse, Visible Technologies, and UCDS, suggests that a "point person" from the board, most likely the chair, connect with the CEO to set the agenda each quarter. Other board members can add to the effort through the chair, a tactic that allows for full participation without putting the CEO on the spot to field individual inquiries or suggestions.

Liane Pelletier says her board identifies a "theme" for each quarterly meeting. "This was helpful to the board since it assured we address each of the key board accountabilities (documented in our 'powers of the board') over the course of the year; this was also helpful to the CEO who could approach each board meeting knowing how we planned to use our time."

Carol Nelson, a director of Washington State Department of Revenue and Seattle University, recommends the use of an Agenda Map to ensure that important topics and recurring items are scheduled: "The Agenda Map serves as a framework to ensure that nothing falls through the cracks and that we fulfill our fiduciary duties. It can also be used as routine way to schedule topics that otherwise might be viewed as threatening, such as annual performance reviews and succession planning."

Susan Rector, a director of Peoples Bancorp, Inc. and the National Association of Peoples Bank, finds it effective to start every board meeting with an executive session: "This sets the stage and provides context for more thorough and robust discussions with management. And it's a good time to find out what each board member is thinking — and why — about particular issues. It sometime gives a voice to the elephant in the room, a subject that has broached. Our experience has been that we now have less need to follow up with management after the board meeting."

Zelma Acosta-Rubio, General Counsel, Board's Secretary and a director of Corporate Affairs/CSR at Banco Interbacional del Perú - Interbank, and a director of La Fiduciaria, Intertítulos, Churromania, ProMujer Perú and Vida Perú, says that once the board approves the strategy and budget, the board's secretary and management should prepare two 12-month calendar agendas, one for strategic initiatives (to keep the board abreast of developments and management execution), and one for compliance (to ensure that required regulatory reports are scheduled and relevant documents are prepared and delivered five days before the board meeting).

Given these best practices, it's clear that the "old school" type of board meeting — characterized by long presentations from management — is giving way to dynamic, focused, issues-driven discussions which leverage the directors' expertise and experience, thereby increasing the value they bring to the enterprise.

"Board agendas are often so packed there is little time for open conversation. We've found value in planning for a time period at the end of the board meeting for 'no specific topic' discussions with the CEO and for 'board only' discussions when we can reflect and think ahead."

Nancy Tuor Moore | retired Group President and director of CH2M HILL, a director of Keller Plc, and on the board of governors of Colorado State University

SAMPLE ANNUAL TOPICS CALENDAR

	Q2 – August	**Q3 – November**	**Q4 – February**	**Q1 – May**
Meeting Topics	Auditor Independent Review Partner Presentation Internal Audit Project Update Prior Internal Audit Project Follow up SOX Update	Tax Compliance Engagement Approval Divisional Accounting Organizational Chart Update Information Systems Project Update SOX Update	Review Audit Findings SOX Update Information Systems Risk Update Internal Audit Project Review	Tax Partner Presentation Auditor Management Letter Review Information Systems Project Update Budgeting / Financial Analysis Update
"Must-Dos"	Annual Calendar of Topics	Audit Committee Evaluation	Recommend External Auditors & Engagement Approval Recommend Internal Auditors non 404 Engagement Approval Non Audit Fees Approval Guideliness	Auditor Independence & Internal Quality Control Review External Audit Plan for Year Internal Audit & 404 Plan for Year Internal Audit and Audit Committee Charter Review

SAMPLE CALENDAR BOARD TOPICS FOR MEETINGS, MULTIDIVISIONAL CORPORATION

February	April	June Annual Meeting	July	October	November Budget
Legal update	Proxy and annual report resolutions	Annual meeting	U S eCommerce review*	Intl Cosmetics review*	Budget for new FY
YE financial review by reporting unit	Resorts Division review*	Confirm board, committee and officer assignments	U S eCommerce review*	Transportation Division review*	Strategic planning†
Annual meeting and related proxy discussion	Enterprise risk mgmt†	Set next year's meeting dates	Approval of audit engagement	Succession planning†	Strategic alternatives for investment†
D&O policy review	Branding and digital investment review**	Retail Division review*	Board evaluation	Outside speaker	IT review**
10-K discussion					
IP protection review**					

*   Business review
** Functional review
†   Strategic review
Source: Cynthia Cohen

203

A PLACE IN THE WORLD: CREATING A STRATEGY

"However glorious an action in itself, it ought not to pass for great if it be not the effect of wisdom and intention."

– Francois de La Rochefoucauld

When it comes to the importance of strategy to a board, Suzy Walton, PhD, sets the table: "The company must be under no illusion: While management is responsible for delivering the strategy, it's the board that owns it. Strategy is a board's most difficult responsibility, and many companies fall down here."

Being systematic and thorough is fundamentally important. "The board should receive comprehensive, yet concise, materials far enough in advance of the strategy session to ensure proper ideation," says Barbara Duganier, a director of Buckeye Partners, L.P. and a director and National Board Chair of Genesys Works. "This package should include a view of the industry, of the company's competitors and customers, and of how the company is viewed across many dimensions. External advisors can add a helpful perspective. The strategy itself should be incorporated into the company's play book, by business unit. A strategy refresh should be the first step in the budgeting cycle."

Val Rahmani, a director of Teradici Corporation and Decooda International, Inc., recommends an annual, two-day strategy meeting when the board can work with the CEO to identify the company's goals and challenges for the coming year (and beyond), and then define the actions needed to achieve success: "We might cover transitioning the business model, or building better HR plans, or tightening up controls. Of course, things change as the year moves along, and we reserve the right to modify the agendas. As it makes sense, we research topics and come to meetings with thoughtful insights. In this way, the meetings become real discussions, with each of us bringing substantive points of view. Because materials are received in advance, we're able to keep presentations quite short and allow time for full discussions."

Another practical suggestion comes from Judi North: "Directors should attend industry events and conferences; that's a good way to see competitors in action, meet customers, and hear differing viewpoints from market leaders."

In *Directors & Boards,* Tom Coyne, Consultant and Author at Britten Coyne Partners, suggests that directors make sure the strategy adequately addresses seven issues: 1) the company's purpose, 2) assumptions about the future of the environment, 3) the company's 'strategic concept' and goals, 4) the resources that are or will be available to achieve these goals, 5) plans that show how these resources will be employed, 6) metrics that will be used to monitor progress and indicators that will trigger significant adaptation of the base plan, and 7) the risks and uncertainties associated with the strategy and how these will be managed.

"A board's role is not only to approve the company's strategy, but also to work with management on its development, execution, progress, and results. Planning without successful execution is more a dream than a reality, and a strong and dedicated board embraces all aspects of the strategic process."

Margaret Pederson | President of Amirexx, a director of Viad, Xamax Industries, and TextureMedia, Inc., and an advisory board member of WCD

ACTION TIPS

To create a strategy that maximizes shareholder value, go beyond the data provided by management to understand factors that could derail strategy's success. Here are questions you can ask to delve deeper into the thinking behind the strategic vision and talent management:

Is the existing strategy the right fit in the face of social and political trends?

What leading indicators did management consider?

What other options or paths were debated?

Are the right talent and right resources in place to execute the strategy?

Do we have the right strategy to attain and retain the talent we need?

What metrics are being used to track the strategy's execution?

Do we have access to relevant executives with insight into the strategy's execution?

HOT TOPICS

**Members of WomenCorporateDirectors say these are the
strategic imperatives for today's board:**

Embrace opportunities to expand globally

Many US-based companies still focus on local, regional, or national markets. But the importance of a global perspective is apparent in buying materials from abroad, outsourcing work overseas, and selling to developed or emerging countries. Directors with experience and contacts in targeted markets can provide valuable input and reduce unnecessary risks.

Participate in the digital and mobile worlds

Social media, digital influence, and mobile connections are not just something young people do in their spare time. Facebook now has 1.2 billion users, making it the third largest "country" (after China and India in headcount). Ninety percent or more of people own mobile phones in the US (91 percent), Jordan (95 percent), China (95 percent), Russia (94 percent), Chile (91 percent), and South Africa (91 percent), according to the Pew Research Center. The "second screen" is changing the way everyone receives and shares information, communicates, enjoys entertainment, and shops.

Explore trends of sustainability and "big data"

Green initiatives are becoming more prevalent, especially in European markets, while "big data" is the next frontier in finding and exploiting a competitive advantage. Small businesses may consider these trends outside their sphere, but they're actually important for companies across size, industry, and geography.

Exploit the ever-changing powers of technology

Technology is a beast with many tentacles, including cyber security (how to minimize attacks and how to act if there is one), production technology (warehouse robotics, exploration systems, delivery systems), and general information systems (for an advantage in productivity, marketing, analytics, and workplace collaboration).

THE ART OF COLLABORATION: WORKING WITH MANAGEMENT

"Coming together is a beginning; keeping together is progress; working together is success."

– Henry Ford

Lucky the board that has an open, collaborative, productive relationship with the CEO and the executive team. Here, members of WomenCorporateDirectors define the attributes that they think need to be in place for the board and management to work well together:

A director needs to build relationships of trust and candor with the CEO and CFO

"The destructive dynamics of defensiveness and overconfidence are the Achilles Heel of CEOs and CFOs," says Zelma Acosta-Rubio. "Their attitude has to shift from 'presenting to the board' to 'working with the board.' At the same time, board members need to come to meetings very prepared, which has a positive impact on management because the dialogue can then focus on the substantive issues."

The board has to have authority over the CEO, CFO, and other executives

Kathryn Swintek, General Partner of Golden Seeds Fund 2 and a director of Turtle & Hughes, Inc., Open Road Integrated Media, Inc., and Mela Sciences, Inc., stresses that board members represent shareholders, not management. " As the CEO is often the person who cultivates prospective board members, there can be a tendency for the CEO to view the board as 'his' or 'hers' — especially when the chairman and CEO are the same person. If the CEO is not implementing board-approved strategies or otherwise not treating governance according to the bylaws of the company, the board has to act decisively."

The interests and actions of management and the board need to be aligned

Nancy Reardon, an independent director of KidsII, co-chair of WCD Philadelphia Chapter and an advisory board member of WCD, tells how Charlie Perrin, the Former Non-Executive Chairman of Warnaco, would keep everyone on the same page. "At the end of the executive session, without any management, each director was asked to comment on the meeting — its highs and lows, subsequent questions and follow-up items. No passes; everyone was required to comment. The non-executive chairman kept notes and summarized key messages. A brief discussion was then held to gain agreement. Immediately after, the non-executive chairman had a quick meeting with the CEO to review the messages, answer questions, and collaborate on next steps. This process took the mystery out of what the board was discussing 'behind closed doors' and allowed management to move ahead without delay on any follow-up actions."

An informed board provides more intelligent input and guidance

Susan Rector says that it's very challenging if only one or two board members have a deep, substantive knowledge of the industry. "Experienced board members know their job is oversight and guidance; everyone should share information based upon their experience above and beyond what's presented in the board meeting. Industries change, new competition arrives (sometimes unseen until it's too late), technology changes everything. New collective thinking is necessary for dynamic strategies, accelerated growth, new business initiatives, and superior financial results."

An engaged board brings experience and expertise to the discussion

Margaret Pederson warns against quick approvals of motions based on management presentations. "Informed, often lengthy, discussions can lead to a more comprehensive, better strategic plan; risks can be identified before they become apparent; new business opportunities can be scoped out. Of course, a CEO might not welcome meaningful dialogue; that's why it's important to keeping the discussion objective and based on facts and analysis. A professional, non-adversarial approach should be maintained at all times."

"No good relationship comes without a fair degree of disagreement and careful negotiation. In my experience, over a number of years and in a number of sectors, the relationship between board and management is doomed to fail if respective parties don't understand their roles. Even when the relationship is solid, it needs constant review to remain effective."

Suzy Walton, PhD | board deputy chairman of Manufactures and Commerce (RSA), a director of the Institute of Directors, a director and Chairman of Medical Services Committee, Combat Stress, and member of State Honours Committee

TAMING NARCISSUS

In their report, "Taming Narcissus: Managing Behavioural Risk in Top Business Leaders," MWM Consulting, a leading board advisory and search firm in the United Kingdom, tackles the problem everyone dreads: Working with a CEO who drives through bad decisions, brooking no opposition; who takes risks that are too big; and who will not tolerate perceived threats to their power.

Taken from a detailed study, here are their insights and advice for tackling these "narcissists":

Start on day one: Prevention is better than cure

The best defense is to prevent the behavior of the CEO from becoming a problem in the first place. That means having explicit conversations with new CEOs on the risks and how to mitigate them, with the chairman setting clear behavioral ground rules and tackling any 'minor' abuses early and clearly.

Build the right board foundations

The board is best prepared to deal with any potential problems when it has the right foundations: a chairman with the independence, skills, and character to keep the CEO in check; a group of directors with the experience and confidence to highlight and address concerns; and healthy board dynamics, reinforced by open and constructive reviews.

Develop sharply attuned organizational antennae

The board must pick up signals on the underlying behavioral dynamics in the business. The chairman especially needs to have frequent and direct access to the bigger executive team; he or she needs to know the potential danger signals, to have the skills to spot those signals, and to demonstrate the judgment to assess when a tipping point may be nearing.

Put behavioral risk explicitly on the board agenda

In Rudy M. Yandrick's book, *Behavioral Risk Management: how to avoid preventable losses from mental health problems in the workplace,* behavioral risk is defined as applying to "the risks connected with workplace behaviors of employees and work organizations that have a negative impact on the productivity of an organization." Behavioral risk needs to be a standard agenda item. This can be achieved through regular director-only meetings or discussions that cover the topic (rather than making it an 'exceptional' issue, discussed only *in extremis*). Meanwhile, annual chairman and CEO reviews should be broad in scope; focused not just on performance outputs but also behaviors, especially as tenure increases.

Never shirk effective succession planning

The board needs to focus continually on succession planning and have a clear sense of how it would replace its chairman or CEO. This gives the board the confidence to act if necessary, while the chairman's or CEO's willingness to engage fully and constructively in the dialogue is a key indicator of whether or not he or she has 'turned rogue'.

HEALTHY DISSENT: ARGUING THE RIGHT WAY

"Great leaders are almost always great simplifiers, who can cut through argument, debate and doubt, to offer a solution everybody can understand."

– Colin Powell

"If the board is suitably diverse then, *de facto*, views around the table are going to vary," says Suzy Walton, PhD. "Each director (executive and non-executive) has to be sufficiently confident to put his or her view forward. But once differing views are on the table, the chairman has to guide the board to consensus. Success is when the directors can see a pragmatic way forward, even if this way might not accord with each of their original views."

Yolanda Auza agrees with the need to be direct and open in resolving disputes: "It's always good to summarize the opposite positions aloud, to acknowledge the disagreement. Then, if a resolution can't be reached during the meeting, a small committee can be formed to work on an alternate solution." When a controversial issue is discussed over the course of two or more meetings, it becomes easier to reach a consensus that everyone can live with.

Turning lemons into lemonade

In many (maybe most) boards, it's the chairman's job to bring everyone together, especially over difficult issues. Val Rahmani recalls a chairman who worked with each director to make possible meaningful and non-emotional discussions. Supporting him, were the committees which would line up the facts and make recommendations.

But what's a board to do when a director is out of control?

Betsy Atkins, a director at HD Supply Holdings, writes in her book *Behind Boardroom Doors* about handling a director who's disruptive: "A rogue director really impacts the board's ability to be cohesive and effective. There's a rogue continuum. It might just be that a director talks for the sake of talking and takes up time and wants attention. Or it may be that someone is divisive and causes issues … You have to handle it just like you would an employee who is put on probation.

You put together a performance improvement plan, and you spend time working with the director on a regular basis before and after meetings to get them to improve and modify their behavior. It's not comfortable, but that's the job. Ultimately, if you can't do that, you have to ask the director not to stand for reelection. "

K. Sue Redman recommends defusing a difficult director by separating what he's saying from how he's saying it. "In one case, when I listened to the disruptive member's concerns without judgment, I found his ideas to be substantive and insightful. So, I started meeting with him before every meeting, offering to raise issues on his behalf; he readily agreed. While this 'meeting before the meeting' approach may not be novel or earth-shattering, it did solve the problem."

But perhaps instead of trying to avoid argument, a board should encourage and exploit it. Susan Rector recalls on one of her boards there was a "designated skeptic" at each meeting, a job that was rotated among directors. That person's role was to play the devil's advocate, to voice the contrary view that might not otherwise be articulated. This can lead to more robust discussions and trigger additional comments from other board members.

> "There are two types of disruptors: One who can't communicate a dissenting view without losing his or her temper or becoming accusatory, and one who sees a different way of looking at a situation, often naming the elephant in the room. The second type should be become a robust part of every board's debate."
>
> **Larraine Segil** | a director of Frontier Communications, trustee of Committee for Economic Development and Southwestern School of Law, and an advisory board member of UCLA Anderson School of Management and Kandela, Inc.

WHOSE SIDE ARE YOU ON? WORKING WITH ACTIVIST SHAREHOLDERS

"When we understand the other fellow's viewpoint, and he understands ours, then we can sit down and work out our differences."

– Harry S. Truman

In the *Harvard Business Review*, Justin Fox, Executive Editor, New York, of the Harvard Business Review Group and author of *The Myth of the Rational Market* and Jay W. Lorsch, Louis Kirstein Professor of Human Relations at the Harvard Business School, ask "What good are shareholders?" and then define an increasingly common conundrum for corporate boards:

"Executives complain, with justification, that meddling and second-guessing from shareholders are making it ever harder for them to do their jobs effectively. Shareholders complain, with justification, of executives who pocket staggering paychecks while delivering mediocre results. Boards are stuck in the middle— under increasing pressure to act as watchdogs and disciplinarians despite evidence that they're more effective as friendly advisers."

For the past few decades, a gradual shift in power has lead to what Peter Galuszka, a freelance writer, wrote in *NACD Directorship* magazine calls an activist era: "Shareholder activism ... [presents] significant challenges for directors trying to balance their fiduciary obligations while maintaining healthy dialogues with corporate stakeholders ... In the past, directors often took their cues from management and dug in their heels, with no dialogue. The results of doing so typically proved messy and expensive."

Also writing in *NACD Directorship* magazine, Henry Stoever, Chief Marketing Officer of NACD, suggests a solution that positions directors as peacekeepers:

"... directors [must] proactively engage these investors, thereby maintaining open lines of communication and building good will. This means that boards need to take into account the concerns these activist investors raise over a company's stock performance, governance practices, and perceived weaknesses in the business operation... a healthy relationship between directors and activist investors does not mean that directors cede complete control. But [it] does mean that directors consider investor proposals seriously and articulate a clear strategy for enhancing corporate value."

In the same spirit, the National Association of Corporate Directors suggests these best practices:

- Establish strategies and processes for engaging large, long-term shareholders in dialogue about issues pertaining to the company's future and corporate governance.
- Implement a program of shareholder communication that includes comprehensive and publicly available disclosures about important issues.
- Include as topics for discussion major, fundamental issues involving corporate strategy, as well as governance (we'd add environmental concerns to that list).
- Appoint one director who would act as the primary contact between shareholders and a committee that includes the corporate secretary or other management appointee, and at least one independent director.
- Develop policies for all types of communication channels, including in-person meetings, telephone, e-mail, and social media.
- Keep all communications policies and practices current.

Madeleine Albright captured the heart of good communication when she said: "No matter what message you are about to deliver, whether it is holding out a hand of friendship or making clear that you disapprove of something, the person sitting across the table is a human being, so the goal is to always establish common ground."

SEEING AROUND CORNERS: GLOBAL RISK MANAGEMENT

"Risk comes from not knowing what you're doing."

– Warren Buffett

Because of the complexity of today's global businesses, and the potential severity of making a serious mistake in strategy or operations, it's more important than ever that the board take an active role in risk management. KPMG suggests that the place to begin is asking — and finding the answers to —these fundamental questions:

- Does the company have a formal risk-reporting mechanism?
- Are the risks/threats factored into the strategic planning process?
- What is the company's appetite for risk?
- Is the degree of risk tolerance appropriate given global markets and competitive conditions?
- Are there multiple risk silos within the organization?
- How is risk management perceived by C-suite executives?
- Have there been many "mis-steps" in the recent past?
- Are the company's earnings more volatile than those of its peers?
- Is risk measured and monitored? What analyses are done? How are the outcomes acted upon?

New initiatives, especially those important to the company's future earnings, are particularly risky. Processes and procedures should be in place to identify and monitor the risks associated with innovation (see page 166 for a brief discussion of advisory boards for innovation and risk). Research can reduce the risk that decisions are based solely on intuition or experience. Also, a specific percentage of revenue or profits can be dedicated to new initiatives, thereby making resources available without putting too much on the table (don't gamble more than you can afford to lose).

A bit of caution is particularly relevant for family-owned businesses which, while they might be relatively risk averse, often lack a mechanism for saying "no" to a key family member. On one of Liane Pelletier's boards, they worried that approaches to regulatory compliance were too "home grown" and may be out of step with best practices, so they asked management to hire an independent expert firm to conduct an analysis of the company's practices, the tone at the top, the allocated budget, the designated personnel, their duties and what they were measuring/managing. With that report, management identified desired changes, so they had a deeper understanding, a roadmap of improvements, and a higher profile of this risk area for the board.

FIVE QUESTIONS BOARDS SHOULD ASK ABOUT GEOPOLITICAL THREATS

Michèle Flournoy, a Senior advisor at The Boston Consulting Group (BCG) and a Former U.S. Undersecretary of Defense for Policy, answers the following questions from the article, "Five Questions Boards Should Ask About Geopolitical Threats, " published in *Agenda* in March 2014:

For boards, recent geopolitical disturbances raise fresh questions about the growing risks that global corporations must answer while serving developing markets.

1. How exposed is my company to geopolitical risk — via customers, supply chains, cash flow, Investments and reputation?

A company is potentially exposed to geopolitical risks if it operates overseas, depends on revenues from foreign customers, relies on global supply chains and financial flows, or deals with globally traded commodities. Directors should be asking whether their company has the necessary tools, systems, processes and internal organization in place to anticipate, respond to, mitigate and adapt in the face of geopolitical risks. Even if corporate operations and customers are largely in the United States, they may nevertheless be vulnerable to risks emanating from abroad.

2. Does the company have an effective early warning system to detect crises, and is it able to anticipate risks before they become crises?

The ability to anticipate risks and detect signs of trouble early is critical to mitigating and managing the impacts of disruptive events. This requires a robust process for surveying the environment, screening, assessing and prioritizing potential risks. It also calls on companies to communicate these matters quickly to key decision makers. Boards must have confidence in how companies measure and report their current exposures to various risks and, also, how it holds personnel accountable for their roles during these processes.

3. Does the company have a crisis response system to manage crises as early and as effectively as possible, and does it take advance actions to reduce their negative impacts?

Advance preparation for a crisis can go a long way toward assuring boards that their companies can assess an emerging situation and generate response options. This requires not only developing and rehearsing a system for crisis decision-making and communications, but also robust contingency planning to explore various scenarios in advance. While the initial playbook boards use may not survive contact with an actual crisis, the insights gained in the planning process can prove invaluable. As President Dwight Eisenhower once said, "Plans are worthless, but planning is everything."

4. Does the firm have the resilience and agility to recover, adapt and win in the face of unexpected or highly disruptive changes?

Resilience requires building an agile organization that can rapidly adapt to change and still compete successfully. While there is no magic formula, there are some best practices. For example, don't focus only on the most probable events; consider "black swans" and other extreme risks. Companies must stress-test their organization by regularly running scenario-based simulations and integrating the key learnings into management's decision-making processes.

5. Is the company developing leaders who can manage well in an environment where uncertainty, complexity and volatility define the new normal?

Leading a company through a catastrophic cyber attack or global supply disruption is not something CEOs are taught in graduate school. Developing adaptive leaders may be the most important investment boards can make to ensure their company can survive and thrive. Boards must put a premium on diversity, as multi-talented teams tend to be more resilient in crises. Adaptive leaders should be exposed to multiple "stretch" opportunities, varied business situations and cultures, and multiple units within your organization. Ultimately, next-generation leaders must get the hands-on experience, training and coaching they need to become effective in dealing with myriad geopolitical risks.

FIVE QUESTIONS DIRECTORS SHOULD ASK ABOUT
CORPORATE SABOTAGE

Carol Rollie Flynn, a 30-year CIA veteran and Managing Principal of Singa Consulting, which provides intelligence and security services to corporations and governments, answers the following questions from the article, "Five Questions Directors Should Ask About Corporate Sabotage," published in *Agenda* in 2013:

Corporate espionage and cyber crimes cost businesses an estimated $100 billion a year. What should the board know about the company's security?

1. Who is in charge of our company's security?

Responsibility for security starts at the top. Companies often make the mistake of relegating security and cyber-security functions to lower-level professionals. The result is that these responsibilities are handled at a tactical rather than a strategic level. Instead, these roles should be centralized in the chief security officer (CSO) or chief information security officer (CISO) positions. These executives report directly to the CEO and are members of the senior management team. Boards should get top leadership involved, clarify security-related roles, and establish a chain of command.

2. Who is trying to steal or damage our data and are they already in our networks?

Attackers fall into three categories: "hactivists," organized criminals, and foreign governments, all of which can collude with insiders and inflict great damage. Companies must conduct a vulnerability and threat assessment to determine their greatest risk areas, including whether specific threats exist in a particular overseas operating area. Appropriate policies and procedures should be then be designed, implemented, and regularly updated to address emerging threats.

3. What are we doing about insiders?

Employees, vendors, and others with access pose the greatest risk to any organization because of their familiarity with security protocols, procedures, and vulnerabilities. To reduce the risk of insider attacks, companies should have comprehensive policies and procedures. For instance, human resources should have processes for vetting new hires before giving them access and for terminating access when employees resign, retire, or are fired. Further, companies need in-depth access control strategies that cover everything from physical security to the protection of IT communications and databases.

4. What are the most important assets that we need to protect?

Businesses should identify assets most valuable to intruders and then plan a security strategy accordingly. Generally, companies will want to protect sensitive client and employee data, proprietary corporate information, and internal security protocols.

5. What's the plan?

Every organization needs an incident response team and a well-tested response plan for when an incident occurs. The team should be led by a senior executive and centrally managed to guarantee organization-wide communication and coordination. It should also include representatives from key corporate business areas, including the public relations and legal departments, and not just the IT staff. This will be essential if an incident involves reputational issues or data breaches.

WHO'S ON DECK? PLANNING SUCCESSION FOR EXECUTIVES AND DIRECTORS

"The wise man must remember that while he is a descendant of the past, he is a parent of the future."

– Herbert Spencer

In looking to the future, a board should keep this aphorism in mind: "You have to play the cards you've been dealt, but you can choose who's at the table." It only makes sense to seek out people who will work well together — challenging each other, inspiring each other, and making each other laugh. To get the best people for the jobs, succession planning should be top-of-mind for every board.

The annual WCD/Heidrick & Struggles *Board of Directors Survey* took a relatively narrow focus, as indicated by the report's subtitle, "The State of Leadership Succession Planning Today." The survey found that choice points to the importance of finding the right leadership, not just to guide an enterprise in an increasingly complex world, but to assure an appropriate amount of diversity in decision making and advisory roles. The report's stated purpose is "to discern convergences and divergences of directors' perspectives by gender and geography, and to consider the findings in light of the often elusive goal of board diversity."

CEO succession

When it comes to planning for CEO succession, a long-range, ongoing process is essential for assessing internal candidates (for the job and against external candidates) and allowing them enough time to develop. Based on input from more than 900 directors in 44 countries, here are some of the survey's significant findings about planning for CEO succession:

- A substantial number of boards fall short in their approach to choosing their next chief executive. Forty percent of respondents said that succession planning is discussed "only occasionally" and is not an ongoing activity. The same percentage say that succession comes up only after the CEO announces that he or she is leaving or retiring within one or two years.
- Broken down by region, the figures vary widely. In North America, Europe, Australia and Africa, more than half of boards actively discuss CEO succession.

But 80 percent of directors in Asia said that CEO succession is discussed only occasionally. Further, more than half of the survey respondents in Asia, Central America, and South America said that CEO succession is either never discussed or only discussed once a year.

- There is near universal agreement (98 percent) that the actual selection process should not be driven by the sitting CEO. Nevertheless, newly-appointed CEOs should acknowledge the issue as early as their second meeting with the board. Ideally, a board should understand that the key question in succession planning is one of timing: The degree and nature of the incumbent's involvement will evolve as the board's assumes ultimate responsibility.

- Nearly half of female directors and more than 47 percent of male directors say that responsibility for CEO succession lies with the full board. Regionally, more than half of survey respondents in Africa (60 percent), Australia (61 percent), and North America (52 percent) echoed this sentiment. But in practice, only 41 percent of directors said that CEO succession discussions are handled by the full board.

- Boards should also plan for an emergency succession. Yet, only 14 percent of respondents indicated that their board is "very prepared" for a crisis at the C-level (such as the CEO leaving without notice), with 32 percent saying they are "somewhat prepared." Among directors in Asia, 77 percent said they don't know whether a qualified person is "at the ready" to lead their company in a crisis; among North American directors, 48 percent said the same.

Director succession

Sixty-three percent of the survey respondents said that their board chairs rarely rotate; 50 percent said the same about lead directors. Although 62 percent of committee chairs rotate every few years, more than one-third rarely do so.

One of the most promising ways to ensure a full pipeline of diverse, board-ready candidates lies in companies grooming their outstanding executives for external board service and helping them secure it. More than 87 percent of the survey respondents said that their boards allow company executives to serve on outside boards. And while nearly half (47 percent) limit such service to one board, more than a third (35 percent) have no limits, and nearly one-fifth (18 percent) allow service on two boards. Yet, when asked whether their companies groom women or diverse candidates for future board service, only 37 percent answered yes, and nowhere in the world does the figure exceed 50 percent.

Another upside of nurturing executives for board duty is this work can improve retention rates. The most talented executives in any organization are likely to be approached with attractive job offers. For valuable executives, especially those with long tenure, external board service can offer enough of a stretch to keep them from having to seek additional professional challenges with another company.

As Amanda Gerut, Senior Reporter at *Agenda*, argues in the *Agenda* article "Boards Dive Deeper into Talent Development," boards should participate generally in managing the company's talent since having the right person in the right job is fundamentally important to achieving strategic goals and good governance.

A path toward better succession planning

In their paper, "An insider's view on succession planning" published in *Point of View*, James M. Citrin and Thomas J. Neff of Spencer Stuart contend that while succession planning should be considered one of board's highest priority duties. They suggest that succession planning works best when:

It's viewed as a fundamental and ongoing board responsibility closely tied to management development. Succession planning is not just about selecting the next CEO. Rather, it's a comprehensive approach to developing management talent throughout the organization. That's why the topic of succession planning should appear regularly on the board's meeting agenda.

There is clarity about the CEO's role versus the board's role. CEOs who work well with boards on succession planning are careful not to overstep their bounds — providing their views when needed, but then letting the designated board committee or team do its job. The board's succession planning efforts should be led by a director who is respected both by the CEO and fellow directors.

The board and the CEO share an understanding of the corporate strategy. It is crucial that directors and the CEO clearly understand the company's direction over the next several years and articulate those priorities and plans in the same way. Understanding the strategy is an important step in helping to define the specifications for the next CEO, who will help to execute that strategy.

The CEO has an ongoing, logical, and measurable role in the process. The CEO needs to be held accountable for succession objectives that are agreed upon with the board. In accordance with Peter Drucker's long-established maxim, "what gets measured gets managed," leading boards establish measurable annual succession planning objectives for CEOs; at the end of the year, progress against these objectives is measured and reflected in the CEO's incentive compensation.

One more piece of advice: When board succession planning is integrated with a good board assessment process (see the next chapter, on page 230), the result can be a foundation for altering and improving the board's composition when necessary.

"When asked if the companies they oversee groom women or diverse candidates for future board service, only a little over 37 percent of the respondents overall say yes, and in no region of the world does the figure exceed 50 percent."

WCD/Heidrick & Struggles | *2013 Board of Directors Survey*

ACTION TIPS

Julie Daum, North American Board Services Practice Leader and a director of Spencer Stuart, and a director of Seacoast Banking Corporation, suggests keeping the following insights in mind when you're looking for a board leader:

1. Remember to look at the person you want to appoint only after considering the puzzle you are trying to solve. Consider the strengths and weaknesses of the team, where you want the organization to go, what skills will be required to get there, and what interpersonal characteristics are required to operate effectively within the cultural norms. While CEO succession will impact the entire organization, other people's decisions also impact the team, division, or group.

2. Having mapped out the puzzle, now identify the right piece by detailing the specific selection criteria and assessing each candidate against them. You want to be vigilant about challenging red herrings (about age, experience, or ethnicity) that are often dressed up as conventional wisdom.

3. Once the puzzle and pieces are identified, use the right process. While the role of CEO is unique, good hiring principles still apply. For example, it's important to get input from key constituencies and to structure candidate interviews carefully so they cover all the job requirements.

BEST PRACTICES IN SUCCESSION PLANNING

Here are some other suggestions for establishing effective succession planning:

- Maintain a diligent and disciplined process that restarts as soon as a successor is appointed.

- Structure the process so that the responsibility for driving it shifts from the incumbent CEO to the board as the succession date approaches.

- Prepare for an emergency succession by regularly discussing contingency plans and reviewing leadership options.

- Maintain a diligent and disciplined board succession process designed to build the kind of multi-gender, multi-skilled, multi-national, multi-ethnic, and multi-generational board that competitiveness increasingly requires.

- Consider the various means of refreshing the board — from term limits to mandatory retirement to shedding ineffective directors — and determine whether they can help your board achieve diversity.

- Tightly integrate board succession planning with comprehensive annual board assessment.

- Make sure the company is grooming and championing its outstanding executives, including women, for outside board service.

WHAT'S THE SCORE? ASSESSING THE BOARD'S PERFORMANCE

"Distinguishing the signal from the noise requires both scientific knowledge and self-knowledge."

– Nate Silver

You can't fix what you don't know is broken. Winning companies nurture a culture of continuous improvement and, in that paradigm, knowledge is power. Nearly 84 percent of the participants in the WCD/Heidrick & Struggles *2013 Board of Directors'* survey indicated that their boards conduct annual evaluations, with the figures for Africa, Australia, Europe, and North America ranging from 80 percent to more than 90 percent.

But, as the report concludes, board assessments are often empty, *pro forma* exercises.

What would an effective assessment process look like? Certainly, it would show how well individual board members are doing, but it should also put a spotlight on teamwork and board dynamics. In the Spencer Stuart article, "Improving board effectiveness: Five principles for getting the most out of a board assessment," by Alice Au, Susan S. Boren, and Enzo De Angelis of Spencer Stuart published in *Point of View*, the authors recommend these principles for improving the effectiveness of board performance evaluations:

The board agrees on clear objectives for the assessment

This helps assure that board members will commit time to the process and provide the candid feedback that is essential to identifying and addressing potential roadblocks to board effectiveness. Clearly defined objectives and scope also help the board deal directly with non-performing directors. Among the areas a board might want to explore in depth are board processes, group behaviors, communication issues, the effectiveness of executive sessions, the role of the lead independent director, the board's relationship to management, and development of the board's agenda.

A board leader drives the process

The board chair, the chair of the governance committee, or the leading independent director is in a position to drive the assessment process. He or she is well positioned to involve the right people, ask for directors' time, schedule time on the agenda to discuss the results, and ensure that the board follows up on the issues that emerge. The leader should manage expectations about the process, serve as an independent resource for directors and management to turn to with concerns, and deliver feedback to individuals if the board is not working with a third party to facilitate the process.

The process incorporates perspectives of senior management and benchmarks against best practices An emerging best practice among U.S. boards is to ask for input from the key senior management team members — such as the general counsel, the president, the chief financial officer, and head of human resources — who work regularly with the board. As regular board observers, these executives often have very thoughtful feedback about what the board does well and what it could do better. Board assessments also can be more valuable when boards benchmark themselves against high-performing boards in the same industry segment or against best practices in a specific activity.

The process examines effectiveness across a broad range of measures
Many boards rely only on questionnaires to conduct their assessments, which might not give directors latitude in revealing issues or concerns that are affecting overall effectiveness. At the end of the day, the evaluation should answer this question: Are the board's activities improving outcomes for the company? In the most effective board assessments, directors are interviewed individually and confidentially; they're asked to assess the board's qualitative and quantitative performance. Topics can be wide-ranging, potentially exploring board composition and organization, board processes and dynamics, board roles and responsibilities, board/management relationships, and the quality of boardroom discussions.

Directors prepare an action plan for addressing issues that emerge
Boards have to be open to the results of the assessment and be prepared to deal with the findings. This means openly discussing performance issues and prioritizing items that should be addressed in the coming year. Follow-up is typically delegated to the governance committee, which develops an action plan based on the board recommendations. The board reviews its progress as part of the following year's assessment.

TOOLS OF ASSESSMENT

In the *Cornerstone of the Board* article, "Getting the most from board evaluations," Susan S. Boren of Spencer Stuart suggests that a "mix and match" of three assessment tools can help optimize the evaluation process:

Survey: Any survey should be carefully tailored and designed for a specific company and its board, and be constructed by drawing from the corporation's bylaws, committee charters, the roles and responsibilities of directors, and corporate governance guidelines. A specialist extracts the criteria against which the performance can be judged and will be legally defensible.

Interviews: Interviews of the board are often used to gain an understanding of the issues on directors' minds. Typically, an outside facilitator interviews directors individually. Based on the results of the interviews, the governance committee provides anonymous feedback to the board, often in the form of a narrative report that is organized thematically according to key areas for board improvement.

Group evaluation: During a group evaluation, a trained consultant engages the board and the CEO in an interactive dialogue. Working against a backdrop of general best governance practices and the specific bylaws and guidelines for the company, the discussion focuses on how a board can improve its performance. Feedback is geared to setting goals for the board to improve its performance.

MAKING YOUR BOARD VISIONARY AND TRANSFORMATIONAL

Being a director in today's world requires having clear vision of the future. The world is changing every day and a successful director has the experience, courage and foresight to help their company transform and adapt. During the 4th Annual WCD Global Institute, Edie Weiner, Chairman of Weiner, Edrich, Brown, Inc., and a former corporate director spoke about how to make sure your board is considering these changes and planning ahead, "What we're seeing everywhere in everything that's going on, short or long term, is transformational. And so the important thing is to make sure that when you hear things in the board room, you are listening carefully for whether they're really taking into account how transformational the times are.... Planning for three years out and planning for ten years out reside with completely different skill and competency sets. One of the first things that a company can do when they think about strategic planning or strategic thinking, is break out time frames and assign them to different teams... if you let [different time frames be considered] within the same group of people, you're either going to crucify yourself in the short term or the long term. It's one or the other. Something is going to suffer as a result of that. The other thing is that there are certain kinds of competencies in thinking that we may be shorting ourselves in terms of the organization, short to long term. A lot of discussion should be about skill sets. What skills do you need now to deal with the ability to both be financially successful in the short term and look at the strategy in the long term."

As leaders, executives, presidents, aspiring board members, and corporate directors, let's look at board service and governance by forgetting the clock and using a compass instead. Time management studies suggest that by doing things more efficiently, we will gain more control over our lives and organizations. But where we're headed is more important than how fast we are going. In the boardroom and elsewhere, we should try to surround ourselves with smart, talented people who will argue with us and inspire us. Working together, we need to create visionary and transformational boards of directors.

In the following article from the *Boardroom INSIDER*, Ralph Ward summarizes much of the key advice in our book on how to create an ideal board.

6 MUSTS FOR THE "VISIONARY" BOARD

The short-term horizon of many corporations has become an ongoing sore spot in business discussions. However, the "short termism" problem itself is a long-term one. One of the first diagnoses came back in 2006, when the CFA Institute "CFA" (a professional investment association) assembled a group of CEOs, directors, analysts, investor relations people and other business leaders to research the issue. Their original report made headlines for raising the problem, but also for the finger-pointing among the group and outside commentators it prompted. In sum, short-termism was indeed a problem for American public companies — but everyone else was to blame.

To drive solutions instead of alibis, the CFA group convened a new group focused on the role of the board in fighting next-quarterly obsessions. The result was an impressive study, *Visionary Board Leadership*, available at the CFA website. The CFA has recently brought a broader focus to the findings of this report by calling out 6 specific areas public company boards must focus on to drive a long-term, "visionary" approach to governance.

Following is a summary of these visionary ideas, with added comments from CFA Capital Markets Director (and report author) Matt Orsagh:

1. On quarterly earnings practices, the visionary board... discourages quarterly earnings games by management overall... oversees the guidance process with a focus on long-term results, especially from the audit-committee level... sits in on quarterly earnings calls, and seeks its own info beyond that given by management. "One director recalled a case where during a board meeting, the board received a report on a stock price jump that happened that day," says Orsagh. "The board got all giddy about it, but the director realized that such a short-term pop wasn't really germane."

2. On shareowner communication, the visionary board... ensures mechanisms for investor input to the board... builds a culture of "constant communication"

(not just when trouble strikes)... stays aware of the concerns of investors, employees, customers and other stakeholders, even when the news is bad. "Can the directors have a conversation on a specific issue, and are they prepared?"

3. On strategic direction, the visionary board... is actively involved in company strategy setting, and knows that its oversight is a continuous process... knows that an effective strategy must combine short-, intermediate-, and long-term elements... can intelligently defer to management on the implementation of the strategic plan. "Our panel wanted recommendations that were broad enough to be effective, but not prescriptive."

4. On risk oversight, the visionary board... knows that risk oversight is a whole-board responsibility...understands the company's Enterprise Risk Management (ERM) plan... can clearly explain to investors the board's risk oversight role... knows that risk can't be eliminated, and also ensure strong crisis management planning.

5. On executive compensation, the visionary board...works to align pay with long-term performance... knows what role risk-taking plays in the reward structure throughout the company... can communicate the board's compensation philosophy well to shareholders, and is active in prepping the Compensation Disclosure and Analysis (CD&A).

6. On company and board culture, the visionary board... asks hard questions of itself and management... is aware of the "soft issues" culture of the company, and regularly interacts with employees below the top management level... wants to know about issues raised in ethics hotline complaints... is intellectually curious about the company. "One of the most interesting aspects of our report was the cultural part," notes Orsagh. "It's studied the least, but, in talking to investors, it's what they find most interesting. They said it was enlightening to have conversations with board members on culture. Directors are coached on things like compensation and strategy, but their comments on company and board culture are outside of what's prepared for them, and give insight."

IF YOU'RE NOT HAVING FUN, YOU'RE DOING IT WRONG

"A person without a sense of humor is like a wagon without springs. It's jolted by every pebble on the road."

– Henry Ward Beecher

Evelyn Dilsaver describes her experience of the lighter side of the board experience: "When I was being interviewed to serve on the board of a mutual fund — a board where I'd be the only woman — I was asked, 'So, why do you want to join this board?' And I said, 'I want to have fun' — if you can't have fun on a board, it's not worth joining. The chair of the nominating committee responded, 'Well, can you have fun with six old men?' and I said, 'Definitely.' The following year, the board had an opening, and I suggested that we bring on another woman. The same chair said, 'You and I don't look at the numbers any differently, do we, just because you're a woman?' And I said, 'No, it's more than that. It's not just how women look at the numbers, but how we look at the culture of the company; we bring up issues that men do not, issues that have nothing to do with the numbers, but that are really, really important.' So, we invited another woman to join the board."

A CALL TO ACTION

"The future belongs to those who believe in the beauty of their dreams."

— Eleanor Roosevelt

We live in an age where education, empathy, and social sensitivity are increasingly valued and where women with their adaptability, people skills, intelligence, and long-term focus are shaping society in the modern world. Diversity in the corporate boardroom can no longer be some place we are going, but rather needs to be a place we create together.

WomenCorporateDirectors has built a diverse and powerful network of connections, resources, and opportunities for women serving on public and large privately-held boards to maximize their efficiency and impact on the strategy, performance, and long-term viability of the enterprises they serve. We offer reliable information, at the right time, from trusted sources. Our programs separate the signal from the noise, turning information into knowledge.

The WCD network leverages the perspectives of directors from all over the world, helping its members tackle today's toughest issues, stay ahead of trends, and anticipate what's just around the economic corner. We gladly share "lessons learned" by women and men in their quest for a seat at the table. As Sandra Day O'Connor counseled, "We don't accomplish anything in this world alone ... it's all the weavings of individual threads from one to another that creates something."

We challenge every business leader to bring more women to the table. Here's how to do that:

Build the pipeline through advocacy and mentorship. Directors and corporate leaders should identify qualified and promising women in their companies and help them gain the visibility and responsibility necessary to earn a seat on a board. This mandate includes four steps: identify, coach, promote, and advocate.

Assure every director slate includes at least one woman. Nominating committees, executive search firms, succession planners, and boards themselves must commit to including at least one woman on every slate.

Declare board diversity a necessary component of good governance. Regulatory agencies, stock exchanges, and governance communities around the world should encourage nominating committees to secure diverse directors and to explain their board selection process in their proxies.

Turn CEOs into champions and change agents. Engage the men and women who run companies to champion and promote the business case for women on boards and in senior positions.

Expand the pool. Even while developing clear and consistent methodologies for evaluating the potential of board and executive candidates, companies should look beyond sitting or retired CEOs for directors. Executives with expertise in global branding, supply chain, strategic talent, risk, IT, and manufacturing in China or India can make excellent directors.

Provide specific board training. Encourage qualified women to participate in board training programs, and then move through the pipeline of advisory board service to director positions.

Sponsor more research. Counting does matter. We need more research on the performance of global companies who have diverse boards, specifically how they can outperform their peers, connect their strategies to their communities, and create innovative strategies.

Report and write about the issue. More media and op-ed attention should be focused on the business case for women on boards and in the executive suite, domestically and globally.

Refer women to board seats. Every woman and man who chooses not to accept a board position that has been offered should recommend women with the needed expertise for the seat.

Exercise all of your rights as a shareholder. Vote "no" or withhold your votes from corporate board nominees in companies that fail to include women directors. Write to the CEOs, board chairs, and nominating committees of those companies explaining your action. Attend annual shareholder meetings and raise questions about the board's composition. Support shareholder resolutions and seek greater board diversity. Monitor the actions of your mutual funds and hold fund managers accountable for proxy voting guidelines and votes in board elections that do not promote inclusion of women on boards of companies in which they invest. Finally, consider companies' board and leadership composition before you decide to make an investment.

Implement term and age limits. If each of us takes action there will not only be more qualified women on corporate and large privately- held boards, but they will make a difference around the table, in the world, and for the world.

ARE YOU READY TO MAKE A DIFFERENCE?

"To accomplish great things, we must not only act, but also dream; not only plan, but also believe."

— Anatole France

Sometimes leaders not only take a fork in the road, but create one. Such leaders are transformational; they change the course of history. With the world at an economic crossroads, board directors need the courage to see the world and the corporations, on whose boards they serve, realistically. But then we need to do more: We need to have the audacity to reimagine and rebuild both.

The world needs more women directors who are courageous with candor, who understand the need for inclusion and cohesion in the boardroom, and who bring performance, not promises. With that rallying cry, we want to urge women directors to lead as we can and as we should.

Make your voice heard. Directors need to understand the complex issues of the company's business. Women like looking at the big picture before making decisions. And, because we're not "baked into" relationships, we don't make assumptions about the dynamics of the board. So, don't be afraid to say, "we need to talk about this some more" or "how about some more facts?" or "have you thought about this?" Just because things have "always been done this way" doesn't mean "this way" can't be changed.

Build trust. During tough times, board relationships can break down; when there are problems, it is very easy to start pointing the finger. Women on boards are particularly good at negotiating conflict and rebuilding bridges. If your company and board are in crisis, spend your energy on creating cohesion.

Confirm your impressions. Women can ask each other, "Is that what was said? Does that make sense to you?" When you trust someone else on the board — someone who's done the work and shares your commitment to the company's integrity and success — you'll have the confidence to state your case and continue discussions constructively. That's how change happens.

Tactfully ask important questions. Women can often raise topics in a way that people find less threatening, thereby making others more willing to be open. We also know how to disagree without being disagreeable. By the time a woman becomes a corporate director, she's learned the value of courage and candor. All these qualities come in handy when confronting an elephant in the room. We do what comes naturally: Asking the tough questions, but in a diplomatic and appropriate way.

Inspire out-of-the-box thinking. Women on the board can push the CEO to be creative and innovative. They can encourage the CEO to give staff executives the opportunity to take bigger leadership roles, which is critical for moving into higher operating positions, C-level positions, and board seats. At one company we know of, the women directors formed the first strategic-planning committee.

Be a mentor to other women. Women board members should cultivate women and help them become leaders. At Frontier Communications, the four women on the board host an annual two-day retreat with the company's promising senior and high-potential women. Each director commits to mentoring for two years: They meet with the women executives three or four times a year. Above and beyond the value of these meetings for the women, the board gets to know the talent in the organization.

In her fight for women's rights, Susan B. Anthony said, "Our job is not to make young women grateful. It is to make them ungrateful so they keep going." The sentiment is still true. Women directors should be grateful for what we have, but dissatisfied with the status quo because this dissatisfaction will spur the charge for change. We need to strengthen the role of women as directors, the performance of the companies on whose boards we serve, and the use of best practices in corporate governance globally.

We need to move together to create boards as they should be — multi-gender, multi-skilled, multi-national, multi-ethnic, and multi-generational. That's how we'll make a difference around the table, in the world, and for the world.

About the authors

Nancy E. Calderon is a Global Lead Partner at KPMG LLP, a board member of KPMG's Global Delivery Center Ltd in India, and is a senior advisor to the firm's Audit Committee Institute. Nancy serves on the WomenCorporateDirectors Advisory Board and is a Vice- President of the Greater New York YMCA Board, chairing both the Audit and Compensation Committees. She leads a global team of 500 partners and professionals in more than 50 countries providing a wide range of services to a Fortune 20 company and its customers.

In her previous role as KPMG's Chief Administrative Officer of the America's Region, Nancy sat on a number of KPMG committees including the Americas Region Management, Pension and Investment, Enterprise Risk Management, Privacy, Social Media, and Data Management Committees. Her direct reports included the CFO, CIO, and heads of Operations, Procurement, Real Estate and Global Outsourcing.

Susan Schiffer Stautberg is an innovative bridge builder whose unique career spans the corporate, entrepreneurial, media, and non-profit sectors, as well as politics and government, including the White House. Susan is the founder and president of PartnerCom Corporation, an organization that assembles and manages advisory boards globally for businesses, governments, and nonprofits. She is CEO and co-founder of WomenCorporateDirectors - which has more than 66 chapters on five continents with over 3,500 women on over 6,500 boards and is the only global community of women who sit on corporate and large, privately held company boards. Susan co-founded the Belizean Grove and Tara as well as OnBoard Bootcamp, which provides an insider's guide on how to be selected to be a corporate, private company or advisory board director.

Susan was the first television journalist to be chosen as a White House Fellow. She worked for both Vice President Nelson Rockefeller and Secretary of State Henry Kissinger. In addition, Susan has served as director of communications for two companies, as well as founder and president of publishing company, MasterMedia. Thoughout her career, Susan has served on presidential commissions, boards, advisory boards and foundation boards. She regularly addresses groups around the world, including leading business schools and CEO conferences. She has written six books and her articles have appeared in major newspapers, including the New York Times and The Wall Street Journal. Her broadcast interviews have been featured on programs including the Today show, CBS Evening News and The Oprah Winfrey Show.

Bibliography and Additional Research

Atkins, Betsy
> "Behind Boardroom Doors," *Agenda* (2013)

Au, Alice, Susan S. Boren, and Enzo De Angelis
> "Five principles for getting the most out of a board assessment," *Point of View*, Spencer Stuart (2012)

Bart, Chris and Gregory McQueen
> "Why Women make Better Directors," International Journal of Business Governance and Ethics (2013)

Berkhemer-Credaire, Betsy
> *The Board Game: How Smart Women Become Corporate Directors* (2013)

Boardroom INSIDER
> "5 Fresh Ideas for Getting More from Boards" (March 2014)

Arciniaga, Bob
> "How to Get on a Board of Directors or High Level Advisory Board," *Advisory Board Architects* (2012)

Brown, David A.H., Debra L. Brown and Vanessa Anastasopoulos
> "Not just the right thing, but the bright thing" (2002)

Catalyst
> *2013 Catalyst Census: Fortune 500 Women Board Directors*
> *"Why Diversity Matters"*

Charan, Ram
> *Boards That Deliver: Advancing Corporate Governance From Compliance to Competitive Advantage* (2005)

Chasan, Emily
> "More Companies Bow to Investors With a Social Cause," *Wall Street Journal* (2014)

Clarke, Richard M
> "Family dynamics and board duties: A delicate balance," *Directors & Boards* (2013)

Cohen, Cynthia
> "Social Media Intelligence for Corporate Directors," *Strategic Mindshare* (2014)

The Committee for Economic Development
"Fulfilling the Promise: How More Women on Corporate Boards Would Make America and American Companies More Competitive" (2012)

Corporate Board Magazine

Corporate Board Member

Coyne, Tom
"How should directors evaluate proposed strategies?" *Directors & Boards* (2014)

Credit Suisse AG
"Gender diversity and corporate performance" (2012)

Daum, Julie and James Citrin
You Need a Leader—Now What?: How to Choose the Best Person for Your Organization (2011)

Davies, Lord of Abersoch
Women on Boards (2011)

Directors & Boards, www.directorsandboards.com
"The Power of Three" (2011)

Dysart, Theodore L. and Bonnie W. Gwin
"Boards and the permanent revolution in governance," *Directors & Boards* (2013)

Family Business Magazine

Earley, P. Christopher and Elaine Mosakowski
"Cultural Intelligence," *Harvard Business Review* (2004)

Ernst & Young
"CFO and beyond: The possibilities and pathways outside finance" (2012)

Ellig, Janice Reals and Kathryn S. Wylde
"Boardroom Parity in the U.S. by 2022: For gender diversity, that is. And yes, it can happen — without quotas." (2012)

Flournoy, Michèle
"Five Questions Boards Should ask about Geopolitical Threats," *Agenda Magazine* (2014)

Flynn, Carol Rollie

"Five Questions Directors Should Ask About Corporate Sabotage," *Agenda Magazine* (2013)

Forum of Executive Women

"The Power of Three" 2011

Fox, Justin and Jay W. Lorsch

"What Good Are Shareholders?" *Harvard Business Review* (2012)

Galuszka, Peter

"The Activist Era," *NACD Directorship* (2014)

Gerut, Amanda

"Boards Dive Deeper into Talent Development," *Agenda* (2013)

"Tech-Savvy Advisory Boards Can Help Directors," *Agenda* (2012)

Green, Jeff

"The Boardroom is Still the Boys' Room," *Bloomberg Businessweek* (2012)

Groysberg, Boris

Chasing Stars: The Myth of Talent and the Portability of Performance (2012)

Groysberg, Boris and Deborah Bell

"Talent Management: Boards Give Their Companies an 'F'," *HBR Blog Network* (2013)

"Dysfunction in the Boardroom," *Harvard Business Review Magazine* (2013)

Groysberg, Boris and Paul M. Healy

Wall Street Research: Past, Present, and Future (2013)

Groysberg, Boris and Michael Slind

Talk, Inc.: How Trusted Leaders Use Conversation to Power their Organizations (2012)

Joy, Lois

"Advancing Women Leaders: The Connection between Women Board Directors and Women Corporate Officers" (2008)

Kanin-Lovers, Jill

"Skills that Every Nom-Gov Committee Needs Today," *Financial Times* (2013)

Kaskey, Jack

"A DuPont Chief's Days of Future Passed," Bloomberg Business Week (2011)

Kay, Katty, and Claire Shipman

"The Confidence Gap," *The Atlantic (2014)*

KPMG,

    Evolving World of Risk Management (2013)

Kramer, Vicki W., Alison M. Konrad, and Sumru Erkut

    "Critical Mass On Corporate Boards: Why Three or More Women Enhance Governance" *Wellesley Centers for Women* (2006)

Kristie, James

    "The power of three," *Directors & Boards* (2011)

    "How to Get on a Board," *Directors & Boards* (2009)

Kristof, Nicholas D. and Sheryl WuDunn

    Half the Sky: Turning Oppression into Opportunity for Women Worldwide (2009)

McKinsey & Company

    Women Matter: Gender diversity, a corporate performance driver (2007)

    Women Matter 2: Female leadership, a competitive edge for the future (2008)

MWM Consulting

    "Taming Narcissus: Managing Behavioural Risk in Top Business Leaders" (2012)

Nash, Kim

    "CIOs Say Corporate Directors Are Clueless About IT," *CIO* (2012)

National Association of Corporate Directors

    Governance Challenges 2013 and Beyond (2013)

Ogden, Dayton and John Wood

    "Succession Planning: A Board Imperative," *BloombergBusinessweek* (2008)

Pearl Meyer & Partners

    The 2013 Compensation Committee Agenda: Go Beyond (2013)

    "Paying Executives for Driving Long-Term Success," *Governance Challenges 2013 and Beyond,*

Pointer, Dennis Dale and James E. Orlikoff

    Board Work: Governing Health Care Organizations (1999)

Price Waterhouse Coopers

    "Breakthrough Innovation and Growth" (2013)

Redman, K. Sue

    "A first step in audit committee effectiveness" Directors & Boards (2009)

Richstone, Ellen B

    "Questions to Ask Before Joining a Board," www.directorship.com (2013)

Rosener, Judy

"The 'Terrible Truth' About Women on Corporate Boards," *Forbes* (2011)

"Ways Women Lead," *Harvard Business Review* (1990)

"Women on Corporate Boards Make Good Business Sense," *Directorship* (2003)

Schwartz-Ziv, Miriam

"Does the Gender of Directors Matter?" Harvard University and Northeastern University (2012)

Shultz, Susan

"Diversity" In *The Board Book: Making Your Corporate Board a Strategic Force in Your Company's Success* (2001)

Sobel, Andrew and Jerold Panas

Power Questions: Build Relationships, Win New Business, and Influence Others (2013)

The Société Générale Group

Getting the Right Women on Board: Cherchez la Femme (2011)

Spencer Stuart

Au, Alice, Susan S. Boren, and Enzo De Angelis "Improving board effectiveness: Five principles for getting the most out of a board assessment" *Point of View* (2012)

Boren, Susan. "Getting the most from board evaluations," *Cornerstone of the Board* (2004)

Citrin, James M. and Thomas J. Neff. " An insider's view on succession planning," *Point of View* (2007)

"Digital Expertise in the Boardroom," *A World of Insight* (2014)

"US Board Index 2013"

"What Directors Think" (2014)

Stautberg, Susan and Theresa Behrendt

Selected Quotations that Inspire Us to Think Bigger, Live Better and Laugh Harder (2012)

Stoever, Henry

"Boards Must Prepare for Surge in Shareholder Activism," *NACD Directorship* (2011)

Sutton, Robert and Huggy Rao

Scaling Up Excellence: Getting to More Without Settling for Less (2014)

Syms, Marcy and Davia Temin
"Boards Coming Up Short on Crisis Management,"*Agenda* (2013)
Temin, Davia
"Reader Profile," *Directors & Boards* (2012)
Thomson, Peninah, Jacey Graham and Tom Loyd
A Woman's Place Is In the Boardroom: The Roadmap. (2008)
Van Der Zon, Kim
"Bring the NFL 'Rooney Rule' Into Corporate Boardrooms," *Forbes* (2012)
Walkling, Ralph
"Be the Person That Boards Are Looking For," *Directors & Boards* (2011)
Ward, Ralph
"Your 'New Board' Action Checklist," *Boardroom INSIDER* (2014)
"5 Fresh Ideas for Getting More From Boards," *Boardroom INSIDER* (2014)
"6 Musts for the "Visionary" Board," *Boardroom INSIDER* (2014)
Wittenberg-Cox, Avivah and Alison Maitland
Why Women Mean Business (2009)
WomenCorporateDirectors
With Boris Groysberg, Deborah Bell (Harvard) and Heidrick & Struggles, *2012 Board of Directors Survey*
With Heidrick & Struggles, *2013 Board of Directors Survey: The state of leadership succession planning today*
Yandrick, Rudy M.
Behavioral Risk Management: how to avoid preventable losses from mental health problems in the workplace (1996)
Zwisler, Eric V.
"Corruption in China and Elsewhere Demands Board Oversight," *NACD Directorship* (2013)

Additional Insights and Resources for Today's Directo

Helpful Resources

DIRECTOR DATABASES

Association of Executive Search Consultants (AESC)
http://www.aesc.org/eweb/StartPage.aspx

Catalyst
www.catalyst.org/catalyst-corporate-board-resource

DirectWomen
www.directwomen.org

Diverse Director DataSource
www.gmi3d.com

The International Alliance for Women (TIAW)
www.tiaw.org

International Center for Corporate Governance (ICFCG)
www.icfcg.org/en/board-practice/female-board-pool.htm

International Finance Corporation (IFC)
www.ifc.org/wps/wcm/connect/Topics_Ext_Content/IFC_External_Corporate_Site
/Corporate+Governance/Investments/Nominee+Directorships

National Association of Corporate Directors (NACD)
www.nacdonline.org

WomenCorporateDirectors
www.womencorporatedirectors.com

Women's Forum of New York Database
http://www.womensforumny.org/index.cfm/layouts/ceo-sponsorship-portal/

WOMEN'S ORGANIZATIONS

Boston Club
P.O. Box 1126
Marblehead, MA 01945
781-639-8002/www.TheBostonClub.com

Catalyst
120 Wall Street, 15th Floor
New York, NY 10005-3904
212-514-7600/www.catalyst.org

Committee of 200
980 N. Michigan Avenue, Suite 1575
Chicago, IL 60611 USA
312-255-0296/www.c200.org

Financial Women's Association of New York
215 Park Avenue South, Suite 1712
New York, NY 10003
212-533-2141/www.fwa.org

Forum of Executive Women
1231 Highland Avenue
Fort Washington, PA 19034
215-628-9944/www.foew.com

International Women's Forum
2120 L Street, NW, Suite 460
Washington, DC 20037
202-387-1010/www.iwforum.org

Women Business Leaders of the US Health Care Industry Foundation
1227 25Th Street NW
Washington, DC 20037
202-775-3900/www.wbl.org

Women's Foodservice Forum
6730 LBJ Freeway
Building B
Dallas TX 75240
972-770-9100/www.womensfoodserviceforum.com

2020 Women on Boards
P.O. Box 301095
Jamaica Plain, MA 02130
617-942-2765/www.2020wob.com

30 Percent Club
30percentClub.org

30 Percent Coalition
561-395-4581/www.30percentcoalition.org

DIVERSITY ORGANIZATIONS

Committee of 100
677 Fifth Avenue, 5th Floor
New York, NY 10022
212-371-6565/www.committee100.org

Executive Leadership Council (African America)
Institute for Leadership Development & Research
1001 N. Fairfax Street, Suite 300
Alexandria, VA 22314
703-706-5282/www.elcinfo.com

Hispanic Association on Corporate Responsibility (HACR)
1444 I Street NW, Suite 850
Washington, DC 20005
202-682-4012/www.hacr.org

Leadership Education for Asian Pacifics, Inc. (LEAP)
327 E. 2nd Street, Suite 226
Los Angeles, CA 90012
213-485-1422/www.leap.org

Minority Business Roundtable
1629 K Street, N.W. Suite 300
Washington, DC 20006
202-289-8881/www.mbrt.net

New America Alliance (Hispanic)
1050 Connecticut Avenue NW, 10th Floor
Washington, DC 20036
202-772-1044/www.naaonline.org

GENERAL ORGANIZATIONS

Bridgespan Group
(job listings of senior positions in non-profit organizations)
www.bridgespan.org

Business Roundtable
300 New Jersey Avenue, NW Suite 800
Washington, D.C. 20001
202-872-1260/www.brtable.org

Charity-Channel.com (Career Search Online)
(job listings that can be sorted by job title, organization or location)
www.charitychannel.com

Committee for Economic Development (CED)
2000 L St. NW Suite 700
Washington, DC 20036
202-296-5860/www.ced.org

Energize, Inc.
5450 Wissahickon Avenue
Philadelphia, PA 19144
215-438-8342/www.energizeinc.com

Giving Focus LLC
Resume Writing Services
401-487-4275/www.givingfocus.com

International Finance Corporation
2121 Pennsylvania Avenue, NW
Washington, DC 20433 USA
202-473-3800/www.ifc.org

National Association of Corporate Directors (NACD)
2001 Pennsylvania Ave, NW, Suite 500
Washington, DC 20006
202-775-0509/www.nacdonline.org

OnBoard Bootcamp
917-592-6466/www.onboardbootcamp.com

Philanthropy News Digest Job Corner
(openings at US-based foundations, grant making public charities, corporate grant making programs, and nonprofit organizations)
79 Fifth Avenue
New York, NY 10003
212-620-4230/www.fdncenter.org/pnd/jobs

Social Enterprise Alliance
(information, contacts, and events about nonprofit organizations with business ventures)
4737 County Road 101, #311
Minnetonka, MN 55345
202-758-0194/www.se-alliance.org

SEARCH FIRMS

Berkhemer Clayton Inc. Retained Executive Search
241 S. Figueroa Street, Suite 300
Los Angeles, CA 90012
213-621-2300/www.berkhemerclayton.com

Kimberly Bishop Executive Recruiting Services
www.kimberlybishop.net

Caldwell Partners
16255 Ventura Boulevard, Suite 1008
Encino, CA 91436
888-366-3827/www.caldwellpartners.com

Chadick Ellig
300 Park Avenue
New York, NY 10022
212-688-8671/www.chadickellig.com

cStone & Associates
858-350-4331/www.deliveringleadership.com

Egon Zehnder International
www.egonzehnder.com

Heidrick & Struggles
233 South Wacker Drive Willis Tower, Suite 4200
Chicago, IL 60606-6303
312-496-1200/Heidrick.com

Korn/Ferry International
200 Park Avenue, 37th Floor
New York, NY 10166
212-687-1834/www.ekornferry.com

RSR Partners
445 South Figueroa Street Suite 2900
Los Angeles, CA 90071
213-986-4840/www.rsrpartners.com

Russell Reynolds Associates
www.russellreynolds.com

Spencer Stuart
277 Park Avenue, 29th Floor
New York, NY 10172
212-336-0200/www.spencerstuart.com

10900 Wilshire Boulevard, Suite 800
Los Angeles, CA 90024
310-209-0610

Two Alliance Center
3560 Lenox NE, Suite 2700
Atlanta, GA 30326
404-504-4400

KPMG THOUGHT LEADERSHIP

KPMG's Audit Committee Institute
http://www.KPMGInstitutes.com/Aci/

KPMG Institutes
http://www.KPMGInstitutes.com/

KPMG Global Family Business
http://www.KPMGFamilyBusiness.com/

WCD Thought Leadership & Information

8 Ways Corporate Boards
Are Changing How They Think

"Boards are grappling with understanding shifts not only in the digital arena, but also in the very human dimension of what they do," says Susan Stautberg, co-founder and global co-chair of WomenCorporateDirectors (WCD). "Who their customers are, how to attract the talent they want, and who the competitors are for both – these are the kinds of issues that surfaced around this year's proxy season and in the conversations among directors outside formal board meetings.

"We've seen that, for boards, it doesn't necessarily have to be a complex technology issue that challenges directors the most," says Stautberg. "Boards are having to shift their thinking around people and engagement, but the good news is that discussions around these can spark real change."

8 Ways Corporate Boards Are Changing How They Think

WCD lists eight areas in particular that have emerged as hot points of discussion during the group's 4th annual Global Institute:

1. Rethinking the "consumer pyramid": The billion people at the bottom of the world's consumer pyramid are demanding a completely new strategy for engagement. "Historically, large companies have viewed this group as the recipients of their public policy work, to whom companies donated goods and services," says Sandra Peterson, group worldwide chairman and executive committee member of Johnson & Johnson, as well as a director at Dun & Bradstreet and a WCD member. But technology changes are making this population more accessible to more knowledge that companies can offer. "You can now reach this market through mobile technology, such as providing healthcare education to villages that were at one point cut off. The people there are becoming consumers earlier, and are the middle class consumers of the

future." This opens opportunities for companies both competitively and in their social responsibility efforts.

2. Rethinking your business model: "One of the best things a company can ask itself is 'What if we could not make any money at all on our core business?'" poses futurist Edie Weiner, a WCD member and chairman, Weiner, Edrich, Brown, Inc. As business models are being disrupted more rapidly than ever, leadership should be forcing itself to think about the ways a company could sustain itself if it lost its key revenue source. "This question starts directing you into possibilities that would interest Wall Street and others, who want to know how you might leverage other assets and potential revenue streams."

3. Rethinking who your competitors are: Companies must look outside their industries to identify where disruptors may come in. Zelma Acosta Rubio, a WCD member who serves as general counsel, board secretary, and director of corporate affairs/CSR for Banco Internacional del Perú – Interbank and director at La Fiduciaria and Intertitulos, comments on the financial industry: "In the banking sector, for example, radical technology innovators like Google, PayPal, and UBank, are setting new technology standards. And consider non-financial industry players such as Apple: currently, with more than 800 million iTunes accounts, Apple is well positioned to introduce mobile payment services because the majority of those accounts have credit cards linked to them. Facebook is trying to get licenses in Ireland so that you can actually send money to your Facebook friends from the app itself. If you are sitting at a bank, you're thinking: where do we need to focus and what new skills do we need to acquire to remain competitive in this new landscape?"

4. Rethinking the supply chain: In the U.S., both environmental and competitive pressures are driving companies to return some of their manufacturing back to the States. "These days one has to be able to manufacture goods and be responsive to the changes in the market," says Alice Gast, a director at Chevron and incoming president of Imperial College in London. "Changing over a plant in China is extremely long and cumbersome and difficult,

whereas with our new technology combined with low energy prices, one can have an efficient plant domestically that can change out the product and make something different with the agility that is needed to remain competitive." Not "outsourcing" production to heavily-polluting plants also creates opportunities to "build plants that are more efficient and 'smarter' and conserve energy," allowing companies to take into account what the true impact of their energy consumption is.

5. Rethinking the importance of board education: Directors need to be on top of shifting trends, such as consumer behavior, as much as company executives do, says Dr. Namane Magau, executive director of South Africa's B&D Solutions and a director at AON South Africa and other boards. "If management stays in touch with the needs of the consumers but the board does not, there can be dissonance between the board and the management. Directors need to be informed on an ongoing basis of the environment in which the business is operating, including the shift in trends and needs by the consumers, so that you have that shared understanding and ongoing responsiveness that can make the company resilient."

6. Rethinking how to attract talent: Within the next 20 years, 100 million educated workers are expected to move into cities globally. "As companies are thinking about whom they are going to recruit into their workforce, it's important for them, and for governments, to look at what the life-work facilities are for families," says KPMG's Nancy Calderon, also a WCD member. The "livability" of cities becomes a real concern for potential employees, who are not just coming into the city alone and sending money back home, but are instead bringing their families. "Features such as child care and health care near your place of work can make a real difference in workers' lives, and particularly women's lives."

7. Rethinking what diversity brings to the bottom line: Issues such as gender diversity are becoming more critical in many regions, driven by economic necessity. For example, as Japan struggles to recover against massive

headwinds – longtime economic slump, declining population, and the tsunami crisis of 2011 – the government is pushing companies to rethink long-held beliefs and traditions. Goldman Sachs' Kathy Matsui, a WCD member whose ideas have captured the attention of Prime Minister Abe, observes, "We finally have an administration in Japan with a growth strategy, and a key component of this strategy is dependent upon women. The light bulb has gone off: we need to start to require a minimum number of outside directors on boards, which is certainly not the norm in Japan. The economic and market reality is such that the government is running out of options."

8. Rethinking compensation: When it comes to compensation, everyone is an "expert" – all executives get paid, and therefore think they know how best to pay others. But this attitude can undermine serious board discussion about compensation, says Melissa Means, a manager director at compensation specialist firm Pearl Meyer & Partners, which partnered with WCD in the Thought Leadership Council. For a board to practice its fiduciary duty, "directors must leave that at the door and be able to immerse themselves in the situation of that company. They need to thoroughly research what's going on in the industry and market and with pay practices in general. Directors also need to be discerning enough to be able to say 'this is what's right for us to do here and what's going to drive the behaviors we want.'"

A Discussion with Kathy Matsui and Merle Aiko Okawara

Japanese companies have one of the lowest representations of women on boards globally – the "bamboo ceiling" has kept few women in the executive ranks or boardrooms despite gains across Asia and the rest of the world. But the country's economic struggles, and a rethinking of competitiveness driven by "Abenomics," are part of a push to open up Japanese corporations to more diversity.

Goldman Sachs' Kathy Matsui, who has influenced Japanese Prime Minister Shinzo Abe, and Merle Aiko Okawara, one of only four Japanese women to hold multiple corporate board seats, had a lively discussion of these issues at the fourth annual WomenCorporateDirectors (WCD) Global Institute. WCD's Global Co-Chair Henrietta Fore moderated the conversation, which explored the many factors contributing to diversity resistance in Japan as well as the movement to break through the bamboo ceiling.

Through its membership, WCD explores the best practices for corporate governance across the world. At WCD's Global Institute, Asia Institute, and other forums, the group distills the best thinking and insights around board service and corporate strategy to share workable solutions that directors can take with them back to the boardroom.

Highlights from Matsui, Okawara, and Fore's discussion include:

Few Women in Positions of Power

Henrietta Fore: When it comes to boardroom diversity, Japan has not reached the numbers of some European countries, where 30-40 percent of the board seats are held by women. Japan has not reached the numbers of the United States, where 16-17 percent of the board seats are held by women; nor has Japan reached the whole of Asia at seven percent. Instead, Japan has somewhere between 0.7 and 1.3 percent of board seats held by women. This is a compelling issue of rapidly growing importance in Japan.

Kathy Matsui: Women in corporate management positions in Japan have held at 10 percent over the past five+ years, and even more shocking is the female representation in Japanese parliament, at only 8 percent. Saudi Arabia, Syria, and

Iraq all have higher ratios of females represented in their governments than does Japan. But the good news is that we can only go up!

Resistance Factors to Opening Boards

Merle Aiko Okawara: A cultural factor Japan is dealing with is that many women and men still agree that the woman's place is at home and not at work. But one of the greatest reasons women face a barrier in attaining positions at the top is that companies are still seniority-based, with a tradition of lifelong employment. If all of these men who are competing for ten board seats have spent their whole lives in a company, they are not going to give a seat to a woman, who has probably arrived much more recently.

Matsui: But there are some empathetic leaders in the corporate world who want to boost diversity. They know that there are more Japanese women who are university graduates than there are male graduates in the country. The talent pool is massive, but it's simply not being tapped fully.

Okawara: Most of the women who serve on boards today in Japan are outside board members. There is very little mobility in Japan's employment force; men are more protective of their goal. After 30 or 40 years working for the same company, the prize for these executives is joining the board.

The fact that there are few women in the pipeline in Japanese companies means that they need to be brought in from the outside. But the challenge there is that many of the women actually working in businesses do not have the time or the support of their own companies' executive committees to go join an outside board.

Board Refreshment and Independence

Okawara: Japanese executives – who at this point are still by far male – largely do not favor term limits, which is certainly common in other parts of the world as well, including the U.S. They do not want to be pushed out from their seat at the top of the heap. We as women, of course, think that there should be introduction of more term limits because that will open up more opportunities for women.

A notable feature of Japanese board structure is that not many Japanese boards have a committee system. Instead, we have statutory auditors (two external and one internal) who sit in on board meetings but cannot vote. So most companies do not have outside directors because of this form of corporate governance. While some companies are beginning to move to the committee system, this is a whole new idea for Japanese boards. The Abe government is encouraging the inclusion of at least one outside board member at companies listed on the First section of the Tokyo stock exchange. As more of these larger listed companies comply, there will be a trickle-down effect to smaller- and medium-sized listed companies.

Matsui: The government, too, is seeking change, driven by economic necessity. The light bulb has gone off: we need to start to require a minimum number of outside directors on boards, which is certainly not the norm in Japan. It may sound like we're in the Dark Ages, and sometimes I think we are in the Dark Ages, but we're slowly crawling out of that tunnel. The economic and market reality is such that the government is running out of options.

Key to Japan's Growth Strategy

Matsui: There are certainly headwinds to investing in Japan – a Mt. Fuji of debt and a shrinking population, which is estimated to fall by 30 percent by 2060. But the fact is that we finally have an administration in Japan with a growth strategy, and a key component of this strategy is dependent upon women.

The participation rate of women in the Japanese workforce has risen to about 63 percent today, but this is still woefully low. But if we work toward moving this number to be on par with men's participation rate – at 80 percent, one of the highest in the world – then we could add 7-8 million people to the workforce. More workers means more income, more consumption, more profits, and more investments.

Some people think this jump is unrealistic, and others ask if gains in women's numbers are just going to take jobs from men. But this kind of thinking presumes that the economic "pie" is static. In fact, the pie is not static; rather, if both women and men are fully employed, the overall pie should grow for everyone in society. For Prime Minister Abe, one of the pillars of his growth strategy is to improve the employment levels of Japanese women.

Fore: This is interesting because we talk often about the performance of corporations improving with more women, but this is a case of a country's production and productivity and performance improving due to the participation of women.

Homogeneity: Pros and Cons

Okawara: The cultural trait of the Japanese being able to pull together as a society has worked, in many cases, in the country's favor, as we saw during the tsunami. Instead of the kind of disruption and confusion you see in other countries during a natural disaster, people were very thoughtful, walking around the streets to give people rice balls and water and making sure that others could get home.

Matsui: It's such a homogeneous society that in these kinds of situations, it's easy for people to say "That could have been me." But this also means that when they are selecting who's going to get promoted in a company or who will get a board seat, the people chosen will all look about the same. So the homogeneity really cuts both ways.

Opportunities for Women to Fill in the Gap

Okawara: Entrepreneurship was not really regarded that highly years ago in Japan – there was a perception that entrepreneurs were failures who could not get jobs in the well-regarded, larger Japanese companies. All the graduates of the top universities in Japan either joined the government or the top Japanese companies such as Mitsubishi Corporation or Sumitomo Bank. Also, few Japanese men wanted to risk going to work for foreign companies, instead opting for the home-grown firms.

These beliefs have created real opportunities for women in smaller companies and foreign companies, who are willing to hire the best and the brightest, period. Foreign financial firms in particular have capitalized on this, and Japanese banks have realized, "We're missing out on something," so they have gradually begun to bring women onto their teams.

WCD Board Strategy Briefing: Issue 1

WHERE ECONOMIC GROWTH WILL COME FROM IN THE AMERICAS

WomenCorporateDirectors hosted its second annual Americas Institute, bringing together more than 125 directors, board chairs, and political and industry experts from around the world. This invitation only forum, sponsored by KPMG LLP, explored business in the Americas in terms of its challenges, opportunities, and most promising areas of growth.

For a panel discussion on, "Where Growth Will Come From in the Americas," KPMG Vice Chair, Market Development, Robert Arning brought together Kathleen Barclay, President of the AmCham Chile and Director of Bicecorp, Banco Btce, Geomar S.A., Austral Capital, and Alimentos Nutrabien; Jodi Bond, Vice President of the Americas for the International Division, U.S. Chamber of Commerce; Ambassador Rose Likins, former U.S. Ambassador to Peru and to El Salvador; and Shannon O'Neil, Senior Fellow for Latin American Studies at the Council on Foreign Relations.

The group tackled emerging developments occurring particularly in South America, and how shifting economic, cultural, and political realities are opening doors for companies both in the supply chain and in consumer markets. In this WCD Board Strategy Briefing, we highlight the big ideas coming out of the discussion—and to where boards should turn their attention.

Entering Brazil: The Rules of Engagement

The $3 trillion economy of Brazil makes it a must engage market and the number 1 investment target for many companies. The country's natural resources have long given it dominance in commodity exports, but Brazil's enormous consumer class is an additional lever for business growth for overseas companies.

However, there are some "absolutes for engagement" that companies must adopt when seeking to do business in Brazil:

1. Understanding the paths to influence. The means of engagement in Brazil is through associations—this is how companies gain access and influence. Unlike the U.S. chambers of commerce, which are voluntary, associations in

Brazil are mandatory, and play a vital role in serving as the voice for a company and an industry. One panelist described a typical impediment, "Most American companies think that bringing their CEO down for a meeting with Brazil's president is an easy path to winning new business, but then when the CEO can't get in to see President Rousseff, the Americans wonder why. It has to do with building relationships in a way that is culturally accepted in this part of the world."

2.   Adapting to localization policies. Forced localization in the form of "local content requirements" (LCRs) was implemented in Brazil to ward off competitive threats, primarily from China. But in addition to these state mandated trade barriers are the cultural localization expectations in the market. A key requirement for foreign companies doing business in Brazil is to hire Brazilians—locals who really understand the culture, context and the way things work.

3.   Political awareness. The realities of the Brazilian economy—which, too, has suffered a downturn since the global financial crisis began—have revealed the inconsistency of Brazil's economic progress. The business community has had to operate amid huge pockets of dissatisfaction in Brazil's growing "Classe C" or middle class. Many of the political elite were blindsided by the riots across the country. These riots were in protest of a number of issues, including inadequate provision of social services.

Will the Next iPad™ be Made in Mexico?

Mexico, in many ways is China's competitor. While the business strategies of many other Latin American countries complement those of China, Mexico's strategies compete with China's due to their manufacturing efforts. Mexico has made a transition that Brazil and other countries have really yet to make: moving from a somewhat closed and commodity driven economy to one that's incredibly open and dominated by manufactured goods. In fact, three out of every four dollars that Mexico sends out in exports are manufactured goods.

For the first decade of the 21st century, competing with China was a bad bet. Looking forward, it may not be as risky of a strategy as initially thought particularly if North America becomes a much stronger and increasingly integrated and dynamic economic space with free trade agreements.

A major competitive advantage that Mexico has over its Latin American neighbors is its geography. Because of its proximity to the U.S., as well as NAFTA Mexico is a key player in the North American market. While the U.S. thinks of China as its biggest trading partner, the U.S. actually sends approximately $200 billion worth of goods to Mexico, which is $100 billion more than what we deliver to China.

It's not just about sending finished goods back and forth, but also pieces and parts; production happens on both sides of the U.S./Mexico border. On average, for every product in the U.S. that is "Made in Mexico"; 40 percent of the value added is made in the United States. Mexico is far and above the closest partner, not just for U.S. companies, but for U.S. workers.

The last few years have also seen a net zero flow from Mexico into the United States in terms of people—a similar number coming in as going out. The current immigration debates in the U.S. are based on old statistics; the high levels of movement into the U.S. were from ten years ago and have tapered off since. The reasons are several fold: the U.S. economy, for example, has been relatively weak, while the Mexican economy has fared better. Another key factor is that demographics have changed in Mexico. In the 1970s the average family had seven children, whereas today the average is two children. The children are also staying in school twice as long as they were 20 years ago. The average 15 year old in Mexico is more likely to be thinking about the test they have on Friday rather than whether it is time to migrate to the United States to find a job.

Recent political and economic reforms in Mexico, including the potential for relaxing the state oil monopoly, provide encouraging signals for Mexico's ongoing stability and increasing competitiveness, thereby signaling potential for increased business opportunity in the country.

Alliances Transforming Regional Competitiveness

Economic and commercial integration is an idea that will propel the region further. When there are such giant markets as Brazil and Mexico at play, companies often overlook the rest of the region, but trade blocs are creating pockets of enormous influence.

A number of countries have formed regional alliances to put them in a stronger competitive position globally. The Pacific Alliance member states include Chile,

Colombia, Costa Rica, Mexico, and Peru. The four founding members of the Pacific Alliance combined (Costa Rica joined in 2013, two years after the group formed) would be the ninth largest economy in the world and represents 36 percent of Latin America's GNP. The countries of the Pacific Alliance are discussing a common stock exchange and common customs for member states.

Reaching across regions, the Trans Pacific Partnership—which has been controversial in a number of its provisions including around intellectual property rights—includes member states from Asia, South America, and North America, including the U.S. When final, the Trans Pacific Partnership will encompass 40 percent of trade on earth. These developments create enormously strong pull for investors and companies who are seeking this kind of weight in the region.

This type of economic integration is enticing not only to the investors in these groups but especially to those countries which have enhanced their ability to move goods and services across borders. This economic growth is driving achievement around the nations' social objectives for their middle class. And as businesses in these countries accumulate wealth, their domestic market may become too small for them. Chile is just one example of a country whose companies are significantly expanding regionally. The expansion of the middle class in countries across the region and the increasing cross border nature of businesses there offer great opportunities for consumer products, education projects, and the financial markets.

The Right Partner, Right Relationships, and Right Messages

The companies that run into serious problems when going into a new market often made a mistake at the very beginning. Working with the wrong partner or cutting corners on legal advice can lead to serious issues; choosing the right professional advisors may be the most important decision a company can make.

Entering a new country is the same as moving into a new neighborhood: it's important to consider how to develop relationships over time. As companies plan their investment in a market, the investment needs to take into account time as well as money: getting to know the community, and letting them get to know the company in the right way. Investing in the best possible firm will pay off many times throughout the life of an engagement.

Whether one is investing in a manufacturing facility, a mine or an energy project, entry requires carefully "telling ones story" Local opponents may start to tell their own story about the "outsider company" coming in to "take all our water" or "pollute our environment" Early engagement is important through in person interactions and robust social media. It's not about sending out pro forma corporate press releases, but about authentic dialogue with the local stakeholders.

One underutilized resource for U.S. companies is the American embassy and its commercial affairs staff. These governmental partners bring the kind of network that companies can leverage to learn about everything from local laws and business practices to the "unofficial" ways of engaging local centers of influence.

As global companies are shifting their expectations about Central and South America beyond oil and other natural resources, there are multiple opportunities to unlock value in these markets. Women are a great under tapped asset in the region, and the growing political gains are underlining the power women are wielding in the workforce and as consumers. If Mexico increased the number of women in the workforce by five percent, Mexico's GOP would increase by 15 percent annually—which is equivalent to opening up the whole energy sector. Substandard infrastructure and connectivity issues still challenge the region, but these are also areas of opportunities for companies that choose to invest in and commit to these markets.

While opportunities abound, it is critical for companies to be aware of the playing field before entering the Latin American market. Circumstances effecting business success in Latin America include political strife, economic dissatisfaction, and the "rules" of business engagement. Boards that understand and adapt to these realities can open many doors for their companies in the region and create new revenue streams in markets truly hungry for investment.

For helpful guides and the latest trends on doing business in emerging markets, please visit KPMG's High Growth Markets portal, located at http://www.kpmg.com/US/en/industry/High Growth Markets

WCD Board Strategy Briefing: Issue 2

THE GROWTH AND MANAGEMENT OF MEGACITIES

"Leading Through Uncertainty" was the theme of the WCD Global Institute, which convened more than 225 directors from 38 countries this spring at the JPMorgan Chase headquarters in downtown New York. Emerging from the Institute were a number of provocative ideas and insights around governance challenges as companies expand their global footprint.

An area that captured particular interest at the Institute was the growth of "megacities" (over 10 million population) and how these entities are changing the landscape of globalization. Megacities – and their risk and opportunities – are a factor that boards must grapple with as the cities rapidly gain influence over global markets and demand more from corporations and governments alike.

"The Growth and Management of Megacities" session was moderated by Nancy Calderon (United States), Global Lead Partner, KPMG LLP; Director, KPMG's Global Delivery Center, India; and WCD Member. Panelists included:

- Phyllis Campbell (United States), Chairman Pacific Northwest, JPMorgan Chase; Lead Director, Alaska Air Group; Director, Nordstrom, and PATH; WCD Asia Vice Chair
- Michael Dixon (Australia and United States), General Manager, Global Smarter Cities Business, IBM
- Louise Koopman Goeser (Mexico), President and Chief Executive Officer, Siemens Mesoamerica; Director, MSC Industrial Direct Co., Inc., PPL Corporation and HSBC Mexico; WCD Member
- Neera Saggi (India), Chief Executive, Larsen and Toubro Seawoods Pvt. Ltd.; President, Bombay Chamber of Commerce and Industry (BCCI)
- Annette Schömmel, (Switzerland and Hong Kong), Vice Chairman and Managing Director, Arthesia AG; Director, Kuoni; WCD Member

In this WCD Board Strategy Briefing, presented in partnership with KPMG LLP, we highlight the big ideas coming out of the discussion – and how companies can best leverage the inevitable dominance of megacities today and in the future.

Unprecedented Urban Growth – Driven by Emerging Markets

The number of people moving into cities worldwide is staggering:

- Each week, 1 million people leave the country to move into a city (World Health Organization); each year, the equivalent of eight brand-new New York Cities are being developed.
- 3.2 billion people – half the world – live in cities today; by 2030, it will be nearly 2/3 the population (World Health Organization).

And the cities are getting bigger:

- In 1950, there were only 75 cities above 1 million in population; by 2025 – in 10 years – more than 500 cities will hold that claim (United Nations).
- More than 20 megacities exist today; in the next 15 years the world will have 37 – most of which will be in developing regions – from Lagos and Sao Paolo to Karachi, Mumbai, and Bangkok (United Nations).

Economic progress of nations has become inseparable from the development of cities. As such, growth of megacities has begun to provide opportunities for businesses, but also major challenges – from energy efficiency to public transport to urban planning, and even how to manage law and order among such massive populations. But these challenges also make cities hubs of innovation that can actually thrive when public policy, market forces, and urban planning all work altogether.

Asia boasts the seven largest megacities in the world, with Pakistan, China, and India topping the pace of growth. India, in particular, is expected within 20 years to have 590 million people living in cities (vs. 340 million today). With this enormous influx of people comes the demand for jobs: 1 million young people in India will enter the labor force every month for the next 20 years (Asian Development Bank).

This dramatic urbanization of the region's population has forced governments to think more purposefully about resources and building sustainable infrastructure and services. To continue to attract foreign investment and businesses, questions around the "livability" of cities must be addressed – questions that have real impact on the attractiveness of the talent base and consumer base these cities promise to provide to the world.

Rethinking the City Model to Create Value

As cities swell to unprecedented proportions, the entire model of what they look like is being forced to change. The ancient paradigm of cities that relied on separation of people (e.g., keeping the sick away from the well) is shifting toward connection: families at risk must rely on social services, which is linked to employment, which is linked to education – and all these things must come together for a city to survive.

To make these connections more manageable, states are consciously planning "satellite" cities – population centers emerging alongside megacities that are having their own increasing impact on global markets. With current megacities being stretched beyond their means, many view satellite cities as the only sustainable solution for dramatic urban growth.

Risk is a major factor companies consider when weighing investment in and around these mammoth cities. For companies, the attractiveness of the sheer size of these cities is drastically mitigated by the perceived risks – risks around infrastructure, resources, workforce skills, and, at their heart, how livable the cities are for their populations.

India, for example, has had to shift its focus in its transportation efforts over the past 10 years. Until recently, many of the cities being developed there were planned around the road network, but this proved to be unsustainable and very eco-unfriendly. Today, the trend is shifting to instead optimize and expand the rail network, which can better link the megacities and satellite cities and their populations. And, indeed, in the recent national elections in India, the infrastructure agenda of both parties loomed large, with much discussion among leaders about ways of bringing the country and its talent further onto the global stage.

The Middle East is another region undergoing a shift in thinking about state projects, which has a direct impact on the region's viability for companies. Pragmatism is driving these states, which have strong leadership, a great deal of wealth, and robust ambition as global economic players. Everything from infrastructure projects (roads, ports, public transport) to utilities and communications networks to social services are attracting heavy investment by Middle Eastern governments, who realize they must address each of these dimensions to create value for their economies.

Competitive Levers: Positioning for Economic Growth

The planning around a country's urban centers is increasingly focused on where talent and demand converge. With megacities nearly strangled by their sheer size, how will cities stay competitive? Where will economic growth come from?

The evolution of cities is occurring on both a planned and an organic level. As governments such as India look to engineer cities around industrial rail and freight corridors, normal evolution is taking place – Mumbai, for instance, with its 16 million people, has grown so much that an additional 8 million people live in its satellite cities. China's Chongqing, one of the world's largest municipalities, is creating its own "knowledge city," seeking to build a place that has both the density and quality of life to attract global industry and knowledge workers.

Efforts to shift economies up the value chain to more profitable, high-margin goods and services are trending globally. China is the epitome of this shift, as the government is looking to shed its reliance on the less-skilled manufacturing sector and instead position itself better for the high-tech, "new economy" jobs. And the rethinking around workforce issues is paralleled by a new emphasis on their populations as diverse human beings who have needs and interest in education, quality of life, and health, and who are, last but not least, consumers, not just workers. A more holistic view of the worker as someone who shops, who consumes goods and services domestically, is taking hold.

A complicated task for governments is to determine where cities can differentiate themselves – to think strategically about their competitive assets and what they can bring to the table. Too many cities decide something like "We want to be a biotech hub," but then do not have the structure to support it, such as a university. Or they set their minds that they will be "the new Copenhagen" where everyone bikes to work, but this might be an impossible dream in a city with a large footprint or a mountainous environment. One size does not fit all – cities need to define their unique offering and positioning to retain their population and attract the ones who are driven to that particular proposition.

In addition to having a clear sense of their own DNA – their own strengths and weaknesses – cities need to rethink who their true competitors are. When a typical mayor is asked "Who's your competitor?" he or she often just mentions the nearest city on the map. But a Fortune 500 company wouldn't name as their closest competitor another Fortune 500 company just because they happened to be in the same city. Cities can learn from each other and adopt best practices, but not lose sight of their own differentiated assets in positioning themselves for the global market. And companies around the world are getting to understand that cities offer opportunities far beyond infrastructure development projects, but are a place where their talent increasingly wants to live, where creativity and innovation happen, and where large numbers of their consumers and potential consumers are.

Power, Accountability, and Social Needs

As power shifts globally from Western cities to developing regions, there is another emerging shift in influence around who is driving change in cities. Governments and business are putting resources into infrastructure, but they are hardly making their decisions in a vacuum.

The people living in these cities, with access to social media, are becoming highly engaged and vocal – putting their governments "on notice" about its responsibilities to its citizens. In Japan, after the triple crisis of 2011 (earthquake, tsunami, and nuclear meltdown), the social media use of millions of Japanese not only informed and directed responses to immediate needs but also sparked in the government a complete rethinking of nuclear power and energy solutions in general. While some of the anti-nuclear backlash has died down since the disaster, Fukushima unleashed a much stronger voice especially among younger Japanese citizens – a real wake-up call to the government (and to other nations worldwide).

Governments globally are having to address how they are accommodating the social needs of their population as a whole – not just the workers they hold up as the local talent pool for global corporations seeking labor. There is a completely different set of expectations among the new generation: 20 years ago, farmers would move from rural areas to the cities, just hoping to make a little more money to send home to their families – this model worked for them. But today, the worker comes into the city with his or her spouse, and this spouse also needs a job. These workers are not willing to break their backs in a factory; they want employers to create working environments that are very different from the ones accepted a generation ago. Companies, too, are stepping in to address the services needed for the workforces. In the U.S., firms such as JPMorgan Chase are establishing a national "New Skills at Work" initiative to train the long-term unemployed and increase worker capacity in each local economy.

And it's not only about the workplaces – governments have to find ways to provide all the services the working couples, and then their children, need to create lives in the city. For women in most of the world, this shift in services provides an unprecedented opportunity. Being able to take their children to school and have access to a doctor for their family enables them to work in the city; this job is the key to accessing economic power as a worker and a consumer.

Collaboration and Inclusion

Even as cities think about how they compete in a global world, collaboration is a key vehicle for driving growth. The ecosystem approach – where public and private sector entities put their collective brains to work on specific problems (from creating symbiotic industry "clusters" to sharing foreign direct investment strategies) – is the model of the future.

Developing cities that address both the workforce and social needs of a population is extremely challenging, and many governments are asking themselves: where are the solutions that one city has found that my city can replicate? Research such as the Siemens Green Cities Index is allowing cities to compare their efforts to their peers in areas such as environmental performance. This kind of healthy competition and benchmarking makes collaboration and discussion among cities a win-win for all.

Inclusion is a strategy that addresses the reality of the global consumer marketplace. As people swarm into megacities, especially in emerging countries, many live at the "margins." They often do not immediately become part of the "official" infrastructure (paying taxes, etc.), either because they don't want to or can't afford to. But while they take advantage of the public infrastructure, using services they can't pay for, they are at the same time becoming consumers – paying for things like cell phones (and they are often using these phones to express themselves on social media, even when they are "off the grid"). Eventually, as they become more integrated into the city and its workforce, they become more a part of the official infrastructure, the "visible" economy, with real money to spend.

Ultimately, the 2.6 billion-strong consumer class living in cities – however on or off the grid they are – is creating a significant new opportunity for global business.

The evolution of this population and its expectations for what it needs from both the public and private sector means that companies must dive deeper into the products and services demanded, and rethink their model for expanding into these markets. Investing in these cities is not without its risks, but the rewards of opening up a whole new consumer market are enormous.

WomenCorporateDirectors Launches Family Business Council

Push to bring stronger governance to family-owned businesses, which make up more than 1/3 of Fortune 500

As family-owned and private businesses fill a critical role in economies around the world, WomenCorporateDirectors (WCD) is exploring how best to improve governance and create long-term value in these companies, where family dynamics often complicate key issues such as leadership succession. The new WCD Family Business Council, launched at the recent WCD Global Institute, will conduct a number of initiatives, including:

- New programs for women CEOs and directors of family companies around both the WCD Global Institute as well as its regional Institutes in Asia, Europe, and the Americas;
- Research with executive search consulting firm Spencer Stuart, Professor Boris Groysberg of the Harvard Business School, and organizational behavior expert Deborah Bell to identify specific skills needed for family/private-owned company board service as well as the particular challenges faced by these businesses today;
- Director introductions – both for family business seeking outside directors and for family business leaders looking to broaden their experience through public company board service.

In addition, the WCD Thought Leadership Council will tackle the topic of global governance of private companies (this year's inaugural report focused on executive compensation). The Thought Leadership Council, to be chaired by KPMG, will address private and family company concerns and compile guidance for directors both in the family fold and those companies' external directors.

An estimated 80 percent of companies globally are family-owned, but only about one-third of them survive into the second generation. "A growing number of our WCD members – both here in the U.S. and especially in emerging markets, where family businesses play an even greater role – are asking for a deeper dive into family business issues," says Susan Stautberg, the CEO, co-founder, and global co-chair of WCD and president of PartnerCom.

"Family companies are undergoing a real transformation when it comes to their corporate governance," says Henrietta Holsman Fore, global co-chair of WCD, CEO and chair of Holsman International, and a director of Exxon. "There is a genuine desire to implement governance best practice, but also to learn how to balance this against the wishes of the family stakeholders, who may represent multiple generations."

WCD will partner with Spencer Stuart, Groysberg, and Bell for a global board director survey. As part of the study, the group will explore particular differences and similarities between publicly-owned company boards and family-owned/private company boards. The study springs from earlier research conducted by WCD – its 2012 survey found that a higher percentage of family-owned business (FOB) directors vs. non-FOB directors said that skills were missing from their boards, and the missing skill most often mentioned was "HR-Talent Management."

Co-chairs of the WCD Family Business Council are Anne Berner, CEO of Vallila Interior, director of Koskisen Oy, Kährs PLC and European Family Businesses in Brussels, and co-chair of the WCD Finland Chapter; and Susan Remmer Ryzewic, President, CEO, and director of EHR Investments, Inc., director of Endless Pools, Inc., and William Smith Enterprises, Inc., and co-chair of the WCD North Florida and South Georgia Chapter.

Other Family Business Council members include Fatima Al Jaber, Anita Antenucci, Jenny Banner, Kathy Barclay, Victoria Barnard, Franca Benetton, Lauren Boglivi, Janet Clark, Carol Daniels, Ann Drake, Elaine Eisenman, Renee Fellman, Henrietta Fore, Maryellen, Gleason, Carmen Graham, Sally Guthrie, Darcy Howe, Michelle Jordan, Jill Kanin-Lovers, Liora Katzenstein, Julia Klein, Pat McKay, Margaret Pederson, Barbara Roberts, Theo Schwabacher, Robin Smith, Joan Steel,

Susan Stemper, Marcy Syms, Suzanne Townsen, Corinne Vigreux, and Alison Winter.

"Family-run companies generate 78 percent of new jobs in the U.S.," says Berner. "But the even greater role they play around the world – from Asia to Europe – underlines the value of understanding and improving their governance practices."

"Good governance and long-term value creation are inextricably intertwined," says Ryzewic. "Family business governance benefits from ownership aimed at the generations ahead, but complications arise around family dynamics and stakeholder fairness. Our Family Business Council is uncovering how to best work through these issues to create sustainable and dynamic organizations."

WomenCorporateDirectors Thought Leadership Council Addressing The Challenges Of Executive Compensation

Executive pay has long been in the public spotlight, with periodic waves of pressure to change forms and levels of compensation to address real or perceived social or economic issues that go beyond any given company. Boards cannot afford to appear tone deaf to the circumstances in which they operate, but neither can they afford to blindly follow the pack. Strong Compensation Committees understand and embrace the importance of tying executive compensation to their company's specific business, human capital and cultural objectives. Achieving this imperative depends on Committees that will:

- Exercise the courage to make difficult and potentially unpopular decisions that are right for the business.
- Commit to a multi-year approach, even when initial results are uncertain.
- Promote clarity and transparency in communicating plans, programs and their rationale to participants and stakeholders.

The Thought Leadership Council was formed to advance key boardroom issues beyond theoretical discussion to practical, actionable recommendations. The report, Going Beyond Best Practices: The Role of the Board in Effectively Motivating and Rewarding Executives, chaired by Pearl Meyer & Partners, contains the insights of 23 commissioners who bring a multi-faceted set of experiences to the issue of executive compensation.

What Boards Can Do Now

The report discusses five issues that most Compensation Committees face at some point, offering practical advice and suggestions on how to:

Use situational judgment. Strong, structured performance alignment is important. However, creating real alignment often requires Compensation Committees to go beyond the formulas and use their knowledge of the business, its strategies and its objectives to assess qualitative factors and reach a prudent decision.

Target the position; pay the person. A median pay philosophy does not mean median pay for every individual. Pay decisions should reference benchmark data and the compensation philosophy, but should also reflect the unique characteristics of each individual's role in the broader context of the company's business requirements.

Pay for retention when warranted. Committees may face times when a retention program is appropriate to maintain a cohesive management team, even when the retention is not directly tied to future performance results.

View value creation as a marathon, not a sprint. Compensation programs should align with the time horizons of the business. In the same way that most Committees select incentive plan measures to reflect company value drivers, they also need to set the appropriate period over which performance is measured and rewards are earned.

Stop paying for failure. Executive severance plans can be useful tools in recruiting and retaining executives; they can also be lightning rods that attract shareholder anger. Identifying ways to limit potentially unwarranted severance will help Committees further align executive compensation to the business.

Through thoughtful design, sound judgment, and effective engagement, Compensation Committees can design executive compensation to positively shape the immediate and future success, growth and prosperity of the companies they serve.

To download a PDF of this report, go to www.womencorporatedirectors.com and find the Thought Leadership Council page under "WCD Initiatives" or go to http://www.womencorporatedirectors.com/?page=_ThoughtLeadership

Reputation Agenda for Directors

A 20-POINT PLAN FOR BOARDS TO ADDRESS REPUTATIONAL RISK

By Davia Temin
www.teminandcompany.com

Reputation is a hard concept to circle, especially at the governance level.

Some try to quantify it by share price, business process metrics, or a complex algorithm of risk factors. Others equate it directly to brand equity. Still others, to fulfilling a social contract of trust with the public. And on Wall Street trading floors, traders will often yell out, at the beginning of a trade, "What kind of a name does it have?" as a way of encapsulating a company's gestalt – the conventional wisdom of just how investible it is.

But no matter how you define it, corporate reputation has become one of the biggest, albeit intangible, assets or liabilities a company has, and thus an important consideration for the board of directors.

Customers buy; new employees join; vendors extend credit; shareholders are influenced; potential partners commit; referrers recommend; goodwill is extended in crisis; legislators demand testimony; and regulators pounce on an organization, its products and services, based upon its reputation.

Even Alan Greenspan has been quoted as saying that "In a market system based on trust, reputation has a significant economic value."

Or, as Warren Buffet has said – "It takes 20 years to build a reputation and five minutes to ruin it. If you think about that, you'll do things differently."

So, how should corporate board members "think about" it? How should they monitor, assess and govern corporate reputation? Even more, how do corporate boards create their companies' reputation?

We would like to submit that corporate boards are indeed an important engine of reputation, not just its monitors.

Why? Because the Heisenberg Uncertainty Principle is operative in the boardroom, just as it is in the physics lab: the act of observing changes what is being observed.

Simply by putting reputation and reputational risk on the agenda and monitoring them, boards can change the reputational profile of their company. By signaling the value the board places on corporate reputation that message and vigilance will be picked up throughout the organization, and reality will change.

Specifically, following are some steps corporate boards can take around reputational issues, to change the reality:

1. Put reputational risk on the board agenda. Make sure to put reputation and reputational risk on the board agenda – at least once per year, and ideally more often.

2. Let the board's scrutiny be known. Let the organization and the public know that reputation – and all that feeds into it – are active concerns of the board. Lapses, such as violations of the Foreign Corrupt Practices Act, cannot go unreported or unaddressed, nor can they be tolerated.

3. Establish best practices. Establish consistent best practices at the board level to identify, prioritize, and address reputational issues, proactively as well as reactively.

4. Stress test business processes and management. Make sure that all critical business processes and key management are "stress tested" under a variety of circumstances, both predictable and unpredictable.

5. Review how management monitors reputation. Require a briefing on who in the firm monitors reputation, and how. Make sure the activity is ongoing, consistent and verifiable. Ask to see a dashboard report at least twice a year.

6. Monitor employee and client engagement surveys. Review yearly employee engagement and client engagement surveys. Look for red flags and make sure they are addressed by management.

7. Review unedited traditional and social media, quarterly. Make sure that the board sees news coverage and sentiment analyses – both from traditional and social media sources, as well as the web in its entirety – on a regular basis. Make sure to see not only good stories, but negative ones as well, uncensored and uncurated.

8. Require preparation of a full list of reputational risks. Ask for a full listing of all the reputational risks that are apparent and predictable, as well as possible "black swan" risks. Review this list at least annually.

9. Review the company's crisis plan for dealing with those risks. Make sure that plans are in place to handle every kind of emergency, with every important constituency.

10. Create a board crisis plan. Make sure that the board has its own crisis plan, and that it dovetails with the corporate crisis plan.

11. Engage in a reputational crisis role play/simulation at the board level. Learn who is cool under pressure, who takes the lead and how clearly each board member sees, thinks and acts under duress.

12. Assure that the company has a proactive mission statement, which includes corporate values, intent, integrity, and openness. Make sure that it exists not only on paper, but is socialized throughout the organization and taken seriously.

13. Make clear what the board's expectations are – around integrity, risk, quality, strategy and excellence – to company leadership, management, and even the public.

14. Enforce those expectations by taking strong corrective measures when needed.

15. Hold one another, and management, accountable, and make reputational issues a known priority.

16. In a crisis, be strong, be visible, be proactive. Assure that management recognizes and begins to address and solve issues immediately.

17. Assure that the company limits liability, but not humanity, as any crisis unfolds.

18. Assure that the company becomes part of a solution. Help the organization focus on rebuilding stakeholder trust after any crisis; make sure to insist that the organization becomes known as part of the solution.

19. Assure that the company grows resilient and responsible, not brittle, in the aftermath of any crisis.

20. Make sure to stand in not only for the shareholders, but for the public, in mandating the company "do the right thing" when under pressure.

What Makes Up a Reputation
- Everything a company is, does, and how it does it
- The quality and safety of its goods, services and workforce
- How successful it is
- How it handles challenges and crises
- Whether its default is to "do the right thing"
- Everything it says about itself
- Mission
- Advertising
- Public Relations
- Selling activities and collateral material
- Social media campaigns
- Speeches, appearances
- Everything others say and think about it
- Media
- Social Media
- Competition
- What its value proposition is
- How it lives up to that value proposition
- What it contributes to the marketplace, and the world
- What its purpose is, and how it lives up to it
- The quality, integrity, strategy, and wisdom of its people, processes, and internal and external actions

© Temin and Company

Boards and Crisis

A SPECIAL REPORT BY DAVIA TEMIN, CEO OF TEMIN AND COMPANY

As crisis has become a new global norm – both because of the increased challenges organizations face and the immediacy and ubiquity of public knowledge of those challenges – the board's responsibility in crisis is changing rapidly.

No longer will plausible deniability cut it, either for boards or for management. Boards are expected to know of problems that are brewing deep within their organizations. And they are expected to act upon that knowledge swiftly. The public, shareholders, and media are holding boards responsible for corporate missteps as never before, and therefore the role of governance leading up to, during, and after crisis is transforming as we speak.

On the defensive

Take organizations as diverse as G.M. and Penn State. A recent *New York Times* article, "G.M.'s Board Is Seen as Slow in Reacting to Safety Crisis," discusses several lawsuits filed by G.M. shareholders "against current and former board members for failing to exercise their fiduciary duty to oversee management." A lawyer for one of the plaintiffs is quoted as saying, "They set up a system that is calculated not to inform them about safety issues."

Even the current Board Chair is quoted as saying "the ignition switch recall basically raised the bar in terms of increased involvement." But did it take a crisis to raise the bar? What is the responsibility of boards to prepare for crisis before it hits, rather than afterwards?

At Penn State, the board was seemingly blindsided by the magnitude of the sexual impropriety – criminality – that had been going on for years under Joe Paterno's watch. Whether news of the attacks on young boys never made it to the board level, whether the board was bewitched by Paterno's aura so that they didn't believe any reports they did hear, or worst of all, they actively chose not to follow up on reports they did hear and believe – the nonprofit board put itself on the defensive as never before.

In the end, they submitted a two-page expose of their inner workings around the time of the crisis, in the media, in order to attempt to explain their behavior. And for boards whose norm is not transparency, but confidentiality, it was an unprecedented step.

What's a board to do?

So, what are boards to do in order to prepare for, possibly prevent, respond to, and recover from the inevitable crises that will befall their institutions?

Based on my 25 years' experience helping almost every kind of board imaginable through crisis, following is a list of 10 considerations:

ADVICE TO BOARDS ON CRISIS

Know that the buck will really stop with you. Public expectation is much clearer today than ever before, and places the responsibility for proper crisis response squarely on the shoulders of the board, as well as management. If heads will roll, they will roll on the board as well as in the executive suite, and further destabilization of the company will result.

Thus, proactivity is needed. It not only looks bad, it is bad when boards are forced to act by circumstances, as opposed to their getting out in front of problems on their own. Target's board faced exactly this situation, when seeking to ride out the data theft storm, and back management's decisions, backfired, and they were forced to replace the CEO in response to the furor. Boards that are seen as only reactive to crisis are no longer seen to be exercising their proper governance function.

Rebalance your levels of intrusiveness vs. hands-off governance. The governance mantra used to be "noses in, fingers out." But that truism has now changed, due to the ubiquity of crisis and denial, and the rapidity of communication. No longer can boards even presume that they will be alerted to every issue the public will expect them to know about. Each board must find its own new balance with management on how to increase their oversight to appropriate levels.

Risk committees are necessary, but not sufficient. Many boards are creating stand-alone risk committees (or subcommittees under audit). But I would caution that they no longer look only at risk metrics, but rather begin to include room for anecdotal data and information to bubble up through the organization. Too many stories that could prove to be early warning signs can elude the metrics.

There are many new and improved ways to do this, making use of social media scans, as well as internal surveys and hotlines. But the committee must be open to them all, rather than be guided only by management's statistical reports and data.

The full board also needs to monitor emerging risks. I suggest that a report on emerging issues and risks – some new form of dashboard – needs to be a part of almost every full board executive session. Old issues need to be monitored and new ones identified to the entire board.

Even letters to the board need to be rethought. Whereas usually all letters to board members are forwarded directly to management to handle, the board now needs to pay far more attention to their content, basis, and their resolution. Please note, I am not suggesting here that individual board members "go rogue," and either address concerns on their own, or speak in public on the issues on their own. I am suggesting that the reflexive practice of board members turning over complaint letters sent to them, cease. Boards do need to exercise more discretion in taking these complaints seriously, and assuring management provide a successful and fair resolution of the issues they have been written about.

Do not put too much credence in crisis planning. Even though most organizations have some predictable, identifiable crises, the real killers are the black swan crises that come out of nowhere. Whereas it is imperative to plan for whatever you can, in my experience, most crisis plans are sugar pills to help companies believe they are prepared for the unpreparable. Mostly they are only useful to swell the coffers of the firms who prepare them: they are almost useless in the breach.

The one thing they are good for, and that should be embraced, is laying out the processes the board and management will use in crisis. A totally functional, fast-moving crisis team really does need to be put in place before any issue arises. Channels of communication – between board and management, and management and shareholders, employees, customers, and stakeholders, as well as with law enforcement and regulators – need to be primed long before they are deployed. And the crisis team does need to be trained and drilled as to how to react optimally in real-time to unimaginable, as well as imaginable, situations.

Don't let the lawyers control everything. Of course, legal counsel is critical in a crisis. However, lawyers often want to control the entire crisis response, and boards should not let them. It is the rare counsel who can understand public opinion and response as well as he or she understands legal response. And these days, the court of public opinion truly can trump the court of law, especially in social media and for reputational concerns. It is best to insist upon a great partnership between outside advisors, both legal and crisis/public affairs counselors. They can and do work together very well, but not all the time; it is imperative they do in the time of crisis.

Adjust your expectation of timing. Immediacy must rule. Remember J&J's Tylenol crisis of 1982? At the time, and for many years later, it was heralded as the best case in crisis management. Yet were a crisis to be handled in the same way today, it would be judged an abysmal failure. Why? The company took at least three days to figure out what to do – whether to recall Tylenol from the nation's shelves.

Today, when news travels at the speed-of-electrons around the globe, organizations realistically have no more than 15 minutes to half an hour to publicly respond in some way to a crisis – even if that response is "We just don't know yet, but are doing everything in our power to find out immediately. We will stay in close communication with you as we do."

The board must ensure that management is able to make the right response in real time today, whenever a crisis hits.

Make sure your board is high-functioning before a crisis occurs. Boardrooms can turn porous in a crisis. Any long-standing disagreements or factions on the board will not only severely hobble efficacy, every dysfunction will come to the fore, often publicly. So clean house now, in order not to create a major impediment later.

Finally, the Board can provide a firm moral center to its organization in crisis. Indeed, it must. The board can inspire the right kind of action and attitude throughout the organization, and vis-à-vis the outside world. This, more than anything else, is the board's opportunity to help the organization recover from crisis not only with its reputation intact, but stronger than ever.

In a crisis, sins of omission become equally or more important than sins of commission. High-performing crisis boards know this. They are constantly mining for more information. They allow sound management autonomy, but are ready to jump in to shore up weaker management. They make sure their own functioning is high – and they never forget their dual responsibilities: to their shareholders to keep the organization sound; and to their public stakeholders, to assure their organization does the right things, in the right ways, in real time – in order to prepare for, react to, and recover from crisis with grace, efficacy, and strength.

© Temin and Company

What Boards Must Know About Social Media

DAVIA TEMIN

Someone posts a harsh item about your company on Twitter. The comment is picked up and amplified through other online venues, and the company's stock price takes a fall – all within hours. Today's world of social media is one where the most obscure person, company or product can overnight become a global trend, or a global villain. Is your board aware of the company's social media strategy? For that matter, are you as a director up to speed on the new social media world?

In this age of social media, organizations of all kinds find themselves at the end of the "command and control" model of leadership. Top-down communications, including those from the C-suite and the boardroom, have lost their primacy.

Today, with blogs, v-logs, Twitter, Facebook, Pinterest and social media of all kinds, everyone has a voice. More to the point, anyone can move markets if his or her voice catches on with the public.

Employees have a voice – including the employee that management fired yesterday. Your "like'rs have a voice; your dislikers have a voice too (including all of the "I hate xx company" websites, and Facebook-facilitated boycotts.) Your competitors have a voice, your shareholders have a voice, and you, as board members, have a voice as well. However, amid the cacophony, it is exponentially more difficult to make the messages you and your company wish to convey heard.

Especially for the board, knowing how to communicate in social media (and when it is or is not appropriate) is crucial. A board's workings are historically private and confidential, and a board tends to be heard from only when announcing a new CEO or in a serious corporate crisis.

This confidentiality makes the much more transparent world of social media a particularly challenging one for boards to get right. Directors must monitor the reputation of their companies. They need to make sure that sales and marketing opportunities are not lost. When directors and their companies come under attack in social media, they need to know how to put it into perspective, make the right judgment calls, and react appropriately at lightning speed.

So, what is the role of the board *vis-à-vis* social media? How can directors educate and equip themselves to act as responsible stewards in this environment? In addressing these questions, it is important to be fully aware of the stakes at play in a social media-dominated world.

Social media is a great leveler in many senses. Not only do all constituencies – friend and foe – feel free to comment at length on your company, its products, service, people and management, but all voices tend to take on the same "valence." Some fringe blogger with a select but highly vocal following can be as powerful in determining your company's reputation on the web as your CEO.

Indeed, many online critics, whether they are 15, 25, 55 or 80 years old, tend to sound like teenagers. In the anonymity of the medium, they can be as petulant and nasty as the spirit moves them to be in the moment, as you can see in the comment sections of online news articles, or even on your own corporate website comment sections. Even when websites are "curated" or edited, only the profanity is removed, and the tone usually stays the same. This is the world that all boards are dealing with.

Many boards still do not fully understand the impact of social media, and many CEOs do not, either. The people predominantly holding the corporate reins today did not grow up with social media in their DNA. To those over 30, learning social media is like learning a second language – and they will always "speak" it with a broken accent.

This lack of fluency brings a high cost. Social media today has an unbridled ability to create and destroy reputations at the speed of an electron. Of course, social media is necessary for marketing and visibility purposes, for listening to and speaking in the voice of your customer, for customer relations and service, for recruiting the right talent, for shareholder communications, and for sales. In fact, there is an opportunity cost to *not* being on social media. Today I'm not sure anyone could afford not to be.

However, the social media risk profile is huge. Further, the extent of the risk can be totally misunderstood by corporate directors.

Reputational risk has surpassed regulatory compliance risk as a major concern for boards, according to a 2011 board of directors survey conducted by EisnerAmper accounting firm. Sixty-nine percent of respondents cited reputational risk as the major concern for their boards aside from financial risk. Given social media's continually increasing importance as an input into what comprises a firm's "reputation," directors need to not only learn more about social media, but understand the strategy and impact around them.

In most boardrooms, it is likely that social media takes up a small part of the meeting agenda and sits at the bottom of the discussion items – if it is mentioned at all. Even if it is discussed, the topic is often siloed into a "social media bucket" and addressed as its own separate topic, which is a mistake. The risk for boards lies in the fact that social media is intertwined into the fabric of everything that goes on right now. It is getting difficult to fully address new products, consumers, market development, share price concerns, customer service issues, etc., apart from their social media context. Boards that talk about these issues without addressing the social media impact do so at their peril, and risk missing a huge part of the picture.

The 2011 example of Penn State University is a story undeniably intertwined with social media. It was not exactly unknown that a horrific series of acts had been allegedly conducted by Jerry Sandusky. This was reported in some social media and traditional media back in March and April of 2010. There were even grand juries called. However, the story didn't catch on then. The story started to take off the day that Sandusky was formally charged with the crimes, on November 5, 2011; then it started to get out more and more, and take on a life of its own.

At that point, the board at Penn State was rather quiet as to their deliberations. When they needed to hold a press conference, they did so. Otherwise, they kept their process very hushed, as boards always do.

The students and alumni at Penn State, on the other hand, grew very vocal, protesting Joe Paterno's firing, sometimes appearing to be uncaring about the alleged victims. Everyone had a response, pro or con. It went viral over social media and then spread to more traditional media. Everything became fuel.

The board's action, and the community's reaction, were the talk not only of every print and broadcast media outlet, but social media around the globe. Thanks to the internet, once something is "out there" now, it stays "out there" for anyone to find, anytime, almost forever.

It grew so bad that Penn State alumni were withdrawing their donations, and the board was under serious attack for their actions (or inactions). In defense, the board finally decided to open up *their* story to the national media. In a three-page article in *The New York Times'* sports section, the board offered a frank, blow-by-blow accounting of their actions during the crisis; they said "this is why we did what we did, and this is how we did it." This *New York Times* piece, too, was one of the most emailed, blogged and tweeted-about articles in social media at that moment.

The same kind of social media situation also permeates the corporate world. Take, for example, Qantas. Qantas had a reputation of never having a crash, but in 2010 the airline had an incident in which an engine caught on fire. The plane actually landed safely in Singapore, but someone tweeted that the Qantas plane had crashed.

Since that tweet went so far against the grain of Qantas' reputation, it was picked up by everyone. Qantas' stock price plummeted, and there was huge reputational damage, which endured for quite some time. Once the online genie is out of the bottle, it's hard to get him back in again, even if the genie is false.

These are just two stories out of thousands. And they will happen more and more frequently.

As social media is, essentially, "uncontrollable," guidance and leadership from the top become the highest necessity. Given the significant reputational risk (and the very real financial implications), the board needs to insist that their company has a high-level, thorough, and frequently updated social media strategy and policy.

A company-wide social media strategy should address the goals of engagement, as well as who in the C-suite has ultimate responsibility. It should also cover how social media will support the company's brand, and brand messages. It should address how various sectors of the company will work together to allow "in-the-moment" creativity required for effectiveness. Yet this creativity must also reinforce the common message, allowing little dissonance in what the company itself puts forth.

Critical in a social media strategy is how the company will monitor its online brand. What is the company saying about itself, and how effective is it? What are others saying about the company and its products? What impact are those conversations having on all key constituencies? Finally, how can the company respond, when response is called for?

These questions become urgent when the company must use social media to respond to a crisis. Specifically, how will the company respond when there is a social media-induced or enflamed crisis?

In short, there must be an enterprise-wide strategy around social media. This strategy should connect all social media activity with the mission, vision, strategy and business plan of the company in a thoughtful, and not a reactive, way.

The board must then review the social media plan, perhaps assigning it to an existing committee or creating a sub-committee for the purpose. The point is to put the review of social media on the board agenda regularly, and not let it be passed over or forgotten.

What about board members who do not feel they understand social media well enough to understand what a good strategy is? Get a social media mentor.

When I ran marketing for GE Capital, the earliest days of the internet were just dawning. Jack Welch wanted to jumpstart his own online knowledge. So, he found a bright associate, just out of college, who became his internet guide.

It worked brilliantly. Jack got up to and beyond speed, and even set up his own Twitter account. He now has over a million followers, and is still tweeting even in retirement.

I would suggest a variation of this strategy for today's board members. If social media is not your forte, have the company provide you with a social media mentor. Using this kind of tutor or mentor can help directors quickly get up to speed on the constantly changing social media landscape – and learn how to spot both the opportunities and the threats.

Once you begin to be fluent, one of the best ways to learn is to begin to monitor the social media yourself, as well as requesting the official monitoring reports and metrics from your company.

Every board member should begin, as due diligence, to personally review his or her company's profile on social media, as well as the profiles of the CEO, the leadership team, and the board. Of course, a director will also want to monitor his or her own profile, as board members can also come under attack during a crisis.

However, a director should never participate in conversations on the web about his or her company. Given the efficiency of search engines, every word you say is not only on the record, but discoverable in lawsuits, and could precipitate a barrage of comment. For directors, the mantra is "monitor, but do not engage."

The company's monitoring should include what the company is saying about itself; what its people are saying in an "unauthorized" manner; and what other people are saying about the company in real time. A digest of these social media comments, posts and videos should be presented to the board on a monthly basis, along with a diagnostic "sentiment analysis" of how this impacts the company. (There are some very sophisticated products out there that can help with this.)

If there are errors out in social media, there must be a plan to respond in real time. The board should also be presented with a regular analysis of how competitors are faring in social media, including any opportunities and threats therein.

When the company is in crisis, boards should request a weekly or even daily digest of social media response, along with the regular media monitoring. The more social media "literate" the board is, the more insightful its response can be, and the easier it can fulfill its governance role.

Develop a "thick skin" both for the company and yourself. Your name could be bandied about the social media web simply because you are a director. Anyone with an axe to grind, a lawsuit, or a real complaint could invoke your name. It can be highly uncomfortable to read about yourself, and excruciating to read untruths associated with your name. You may even feel compelled to jump in to "correct the record." That would, in general, be a mistake.

Any words you post will always be on the record, forever. They will be scrutinized by professional contacts, competitors, customers, the media, critics, class-action lawyers, you name it. It is all discoverable.

This is happening to all of us. Remember, you are an audience of one among billions of other audiences of one. You will see a specialized feed of postings about you when you Google yourself that most others in the world will not see. It will all seem personal to you, and disproportional. However, remember to put this into context and develop a thick skin.

That said, the company should protect you to the best of its ability from scurrilous social media attacks. There are a portfolio of tactics to deploy, and crisis managers should be adept at calming down the situation. It is certainly within a director's right to request such help, either from the company's social media head or an outside expert, should a nasty situation arise.

In sum, the role of a director is to become an informed observer of social media, able to exercise your governance role by monitoring activity, reviewing strategy, and making wise decisions at the speed of the internet. Directors are forging best practices around social media in real time. The medium may change, but the practices of good corporate governance do not.

WomenCorporateDirectors (WCD) Fact Sheet

VISION

WomenCorporateDirectors (WCD) is the only global membership organization and community of women corporate directors. In this new era of responsibility, WCD is committed to not just good governance, but to governance with global vision. Smart boards are going global in members and mindset. Our members share information and insights in order to ensure best practices in corporate governance around the world. The combined market capitalization of the companies on whose boards the WCD members serve totals almost $8 trillion; if WCD were a country, its economy would be the world's third largest, behind only the U.S. and China.

WCD acts as a bold catalyst for thought leadership, networking, and new relationships. WCD is a true champion for women directors and a vital source of governance expertise. Not only has WCD developed a trusted community for advice and experience to help women directors share best practices and learn from this valuable network, but WCD has also helped secure board and advisory board positions for numerous women around the world.

WCD has connected women directors globally to form a network of powerful and influential decision makers. Our mission is to continue to enrich the WCD community through leadership, diversity of thought and experience, education, and best practices in corporate governance. WCD fosters our international network by providing an intimate and trusted community to learn, brainstorm and problem-solve global issues. Local, regional, national, and international WCD forums generate candid, thoughtful, and confidential dialogue on issues facing directors and their companies. Through the process of learning from each other, WCD helps members navigate the challenges of conducting business in a highly competitive and volatile global economy.

In the 21st century, directors must not only develop a company's global strategy, but also be vigilant watchdogs who understand the hidden challenges of working around the globe. Corporate Governance today demands a world view. Boards need the right leaders, to adequately analyze risk, to have the in-depth knowledge of their companies' operations, and to help management see beyond the next quarter to the bigger picture, regardless of the market. WCD is a network than can leverage local, regional, and global knowledge and perspective from other directors and boards worldwide.

WHO WE ARE

WCD members are among the world's most powerful and influential business women—the global business elite.

WCD was founded by Susan Stautberg the President of PartnerCom Corporation, which creates and manages Advisory Boards globally, and later joined by Alison Winter, former President and CEO, Personal Financial Services – Northeast for Northern Trust, and Director of Nordstrom, who became a Co-Founder. Henrietta Fore, Chairman of the Board and CEO of Holsman International, former Administrator of USAID, Director of Exxon Mobil Corporation and Theravance, Inc., and Co-Chair of the Asia Society, has joined as a Global Co-Chair.

Members serve as directors of global Stock Exchanges. WCD members are very senior, influential executives (Chairmen, CEO's, COO's and other C-level executives).WCD's standard is that members are directors of public or large private company boards. A small number of members have or will soon serve on public boards and currently serve on private, mutual funds or major non-profit boards.

WCD's Global Partner (KPMG); Premier Partner (Spencer Stuart); Strategic Partners (Marriott International, Marsh & McLennan Companies, Pearl Meyers & Partners); and Alliance Partners (IFC, JPMorgan Chase, and Northern Trust) provide expertise in relevant areas of corporate governance, succession, executive search, finance, accounting, risk management, and other issues.

WHERE WE ARE

WCD has 66 global chapters. WCD has chapters in **Arizona, Atlanta, Beijing, Boston, Charlotte, Chicago, Chile, Cleveland, Colombia, Columbus, Dallas/Fort Worth, Delhi, Denmark, Finland, France, Germany, Greater Colorado, Greater New Mexico, Gulf Cooperation Council, Hanoi, Hawaii, Ho Chi Minh City, Hong Kong, Houston, Iceland Indonesia, Israel, Japan, Kansas City, Kenya, London, Los Angeles/Orange County, Malaysia, Melbourne, Mexico, Milan, Minnesota, Morocco, Mumbai, Netherlands, New York, New Zealand, Nigeria, Northern California, North Florida/South Georgia,**

Panama Peru, Philadelphia, Philippines, Quebec, Rio de Janeiro, Rome, San Diego, Sao Paulo Seattle, Shanghai, Singapore, South Africa, South Florida, Switzerland, Sydney, Tennessee, Toronto, Turkey, Washington, D.C. and Western Canada. Future Chapters in discussion include **Argentina, Brussels, Guatemala, Mongolia, Poland, Puerto Rico, South Korea, Spain, Tampa, Thailand and Wisconsin**.

A

H

I

L

M